# Modern Match Fishing

*by*

## DAVE KING

*Edited by*
## COLIN DYSON

PUBLICATIONS

First published in Great Britain by
Pisces Angling Publications
P.O. Box 116, Doncaster
South Yorkshire DN5 9NH

First Published – July 1987

ISBN 0 948584 05 X (hardback)
ISBN 0 948584 04 1 (softback)

Printed by Jackson Wilson Ltd.,
Unit 4, Gelderd Trading Estate,
Westvale, Leeds LS12 6BD
Typesetting/Design by PFB Art & Type Ltd.,
4 & 8 Slaid Hill Court, Shadwell, Leeds LS17 8TJ
Binding by Woods (Bradford) Ltd.,


Further copies available from:
Pisces Angling Publications

**PUBLICATIONS**

# CONTENTS

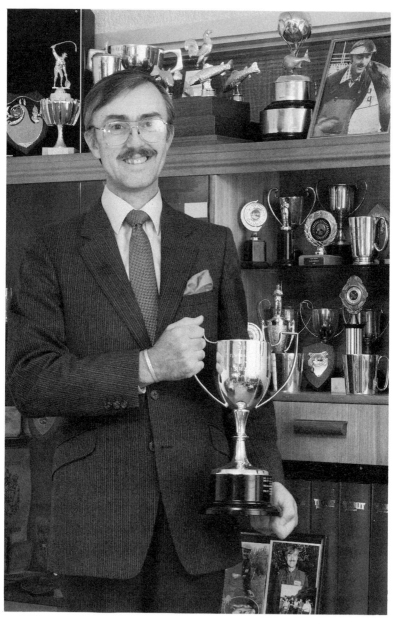

*Ken Giles with some of the fruits of his successful match fishing career.*

# FOREWORD

There is a constantly changing pattern in match fishing and in angling in general. New technology produces up-to-the-minute items of tackle, be it rods, lines, poles, etc, and new methods and baits are continually being brought forwards to be tried and tested. Each development will be analysed, and those that are to our advantage will be incorporated into the armament of angling. Even then, this will not be an end to it. Anglers, especially match anglers, have very inventive minds, and soon begin to add to or adapt the new technology and ideas still further to their own benefit.

When you consider that the whole of Great Britain is steeped in match fishing, with each region having its own specialist approach, and in addition we have the growing influence that filters through from the continent, then all of this can be a very confusing state of affairs. Young anglers, up and coming stars and others taking up the sport will have to travel down this slippery road of confusion. This book will help them down that road. It covers all of the country, with traditional and new ideas and methods being fully explained with nothing hidden, and to the experienced angler who is constantly trying to keep abreast of the times, this book will be invaluable, as you will have a constant source of reference.

Success in match angling can be a solitary affair, but when team fishing it can be shared by all in that team. The thrill that you get from your team winning the National Championships or other major team competition, or of having the top weight in your team can never be forgotten. I hope that many, many of you will have the pleasure of sharing that feeling. If this book can help you to achieve that, then it will have served its purpose.

May you have many happy hours of reading and fishing.

Ken Giles

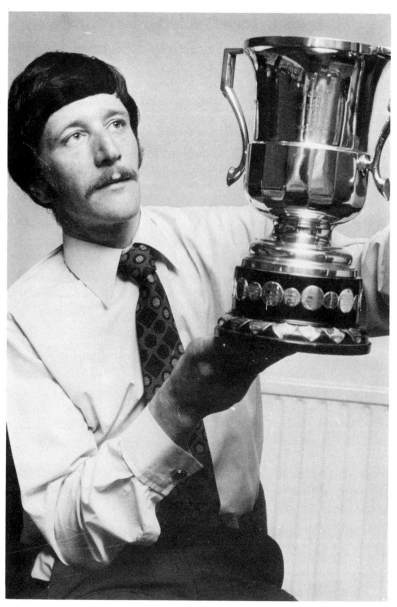

*The author with his local association's Annual Championships Trophy, October 1976.*

# INTRODUCTION

Match fishing can be at many different levels, from a friendly bet amongst a small group of pleasure anglers, to a top class invitation match with hundreds of pounds at stake. But a successful match angler would approach both levels with the same degree of commitment.

Before an angler can compete successfully at any level, he must be capable of performing every function fluently and without conscious thought. He must be an angling machine, the epitomé of efficiency and speed. Every action must be smooth and controlled. His equipment must be of the highest quality and laid out in an orderly and efficient manner. This frees his mind to concentrate on the business of amassing the highest possible weight in the time available from the given stretch of water in front of him. He cannot choose his swim nor the time of day when he can fish. During the summer months the usual match times of 10am to 3pm are not considered the best times in which to catch fish. He is starting when the fish have normally gone off the feed, and finishing before they are due on again – the worst of both worlds. Unless he has fished the swim before in similar conditions, which is rare for most matchmen, he must establish the geography of the swim, assess the potential in species and possible top weight, and then decide upon the best approach having regard to the prevailing conditions. It is here that the difference between the occasional match angler and the top class regular will become apparent.

The occasional matchman will decide upon an approach, but if after a period fish are not forthcoming, doubt will creep into his mind and he will start to panic. Soon he will try every different weapon in his armoury and every possible line in the river. Sometimes this may pay off, and the correct method will be chosen and the lie of the fish located, but this may be because the initial choice of method or reading of the swim was inaccurate. The chances are that if this method also ceases to bear fruit, another method and line will be adopted.

Meanwhile the regular matchman, confident he has chosen the correct method, will be steadily building up his swim. He will feel confident that when the fish do move in and start to feed, he will have prepared his swim well and the fish will settle down and start to feed confidently. He will still feed the same line, and possibly a reserve line well away from the original, but he will constantly change his depth and shotting pattern to try to locate the level at which the fish are feeding. Slowly at first he will catch the odd fish, then gradually he will build up his catch rate. His bait and tackle will have been in the water for the maximum period during the match, and nothing that swims which has been slightly responsive to his bait will have been missed. During the last hour, the four hours of preparation will be paying off. At the end of the match the other angler will be busily dismantling a number of rods and poles. He will have spent half the match out of the water whilst constantly changing methods and tackle. He will have caught a few fish, but at what expense of time lost and effort wasted. Eventually this angler will gain in experience and have more confidence in his initial assessment of a swim and stick by it. He already has the versatility, but needs to learn and control its application.

Once an angler has learned to use and apply the vast range of methods available to him, he is ready to pit his ability against his fellow anglers. The secret is not to try to run before you can walk. As in any other form of sport, you must serve your apprenticeship before you can reap the rewards. To start competing at open level before you have measured yourself against the best anglers at club level will prove costly in both financial terms and to your confidence and pride. The costs of fishing at open level are getting increasingly higher. Petrol and bait costs for both match and practise sessions must be met. The same amount of bait must be used on practise sessions as in a match if a realistic appraisal is to be made. On the day, there will be entry fees and pools to find, and unless some regular return by means of prize money is forthcoming to subsidise these costs, the average angler will find regular open match fishing beyond his reach.

Most anglers start match fishing at club level. The travel costs are low as this normally involves fishing local club waters, or 30 or so anglers sharing the cost of a coach to the more distant venues. The pools are generally nominal, and the whole event is normally well-natured friendly rivalry for low stakes, the pride and prestige of winning being more important than the financial returns. Even so, the motivation and the will to win must be just as strong in the determined would-be match angler if he is to stand any chance on the open circuit.

Due to the rapid improvement of equipment and the free flow of information on methods and tactics by the experts in the angling press, the standard of ability of the average club angler has increased immeasurably over the last five years. This in turn is reflected in the quality of anglers competing on the open circuit. Ten years ago when travel and bait costs were lower in real terms and venues more patchy in fish population, a good angler with a good draw was only competing against ten per cent of the field. In these days of pollution free rivers, with a more widespread and varied fish population, combined with a more knowledgeable and competent opposition, the average match angler finds the odds a lot less in his favour. Fluke results due to extreme conditions still give some hope to the average matchman, but more and more it is the same small group of top class anglers who consistently win, or get places in the big opens.

So it is even more important now to find the level at which you can remain a force to be reckoned with. If you have consistently been in the top three places at club level, try the local association matches at your local venues. Once you have secured a regular placing in section and match wins you can move further afield, selecting venues with which you are familiar and which need to be approached by your strongest methods. If you then wish to progress further, you must look at your range of approaches and methods and decide which are your weakest points. Is it pole fishing, or using a waggler at long range? Are you good at swing tipping but find swim feeders on flowing water a problem? Once you have identified your weaknesses, concentrate on them and practise them until they become your strengths.

The average length of a fishing match is five hours, but the dedicated matchman will need to put in many times this short period in preparation for the event. Before going to a venue to practise, particularly if it is a water he does not fish regularly, he will need to collect as much information as possible about its current form, section variations, successful methods, and baits. His sources of information will be the angling press, the match regulars' 'grapevine', or by chatting with local anglers when he goes on his practise session. Much of the week prior to a match must also be dedicated to the preparation of the bait and tackle. Many of the top matchmen breed much of their own hookbait. If carefully selected and prepared, commercial bait will be quite adequate for club level match fishing. The same degree of preparation is also essential for the pleasure angler if consistent success is to be achieved. Commercial maggots must be sieved and put into fresh bran to remove any grease, and any dead maggots and skins separated. This will also remove most of the odour of the feed from the bait. This is especially essential if you wish to dye your own bait, as the colouring agents will not take if the slightest hint of grease is still present. Several changes of bran or maize meal, which can be obtained from pet stores or corn merchants, may be needed to achieve this.

If you require casters and the regular quality from your local tackle shop is in doubt, you must be prepared to 'turn' your own. This procedure is fully described in the chapter on baits. Top matchmen always prepare their own casters to ensure both quality and quantity are available when required. Obviously this means buying a large amount of maggots, or having understanding neighbours who will tolerate a mini bait farm in their midst.

Tackle preparation is just as essential as the attention lavished on the bait. All equipment must be examined carefully for damage or wear, and a check kept to ensure that sufficient quantities of small consumable items such as hooks, shots, and leger weights are maintained. Line should be checked and replaced on a regular basis, and reels should be cleaned, checked, and returned to the manufacturers for servicing each close season. Rod rings and reel line guides should be examined for wear and grooving, and nets checked for fraying due to abrasion, which can develop holes and cost a placing because your hard earned fish escaped. A tidy and well laid out tackle box will reveal at a glance any reduction or losses in essential items. Regular checks and inspections will reveal any problems prior to, rather than during a match.

As you can see, the dedication and determination required to succeed in match fishing is high, and unless you and your immediate family are prepared to uphold the commitment in both time consuming and financial terms, and be single-minded in your will to succeed, then match fishing at open level should not be considered. No one can tell you how to become a top class match angler, most are born rather than made. I defy any man to define the qualities present in our top International team anglers over and above their outstanding knowledge, tackle handling and experience, but which are missing in their equally experienced but less successful rivals. All I can attempt to do with this book is to guide you along the path to the limits of your future ability.

# 1  EQUIPMENT

The range of equipment now available to the match angler is more comprehensive than at any other time in angling history. The growth of match fishing, both in the numbers and in the ability of its participants, and the involvement of tackle companies in the sponsorship of match groups, has resulted in a vast range of specialist products to suit the equally vast range of methods currently in use or being developed. This also helps to satisfy the widely differing preferences of individual anglers in the way in which they personally approach a method or situation.

## Rods

The introduction and development of hi-tech aerospace materials for use in rod making has given rod designers far more freedom in the quest for perfect action and balance, and more and more rods are being designed using a combination of different materials to achieve this aim. In many cases fibreglass is being re-introduced, using the advantage of its softness in action and shock absorption qualities to produce certain types of action which cannot be simulated by the lighter, stronger, but stiffer carbon fibre. The effect of all this is tremendously helpful to the experienced match angler who knows exactly what he requires to perform a particular task and which suits his personal style and approach, but it is extremely confusing for the newcomer when he tries to evaluate the different makes and designs of rods which all claim to do the same job. Obviously the purpose of this chapter is to attempt to guide the aspiring match angler through the maze, and to try to outline the basic qualities he must look for in the various types of rod he will need to perform specific tasks. But the final choice within the range must remain with the reader, as personal preference is obviously as wide as the range of rods available.

The correct rod for any particular angling function is the one the angler can use without conscious thought. To use the old cliché, it must literally be an extension of his arm. He must be able to cast, strike, and play fish within the limitations of his line strength, without having to consider or compensate for any deficiences in the performance of the rod or in his own style. Whilst it is obvious that individual style will vary from one angler to another, no rod can completely counter an inefficient style on the part of the angler. Badly timed and over-enthusiastic striking will still result in missed bites or 'crack offs' and lost fish, regardless of the design and quality of the rod, although some rods will cope with this better than others. Anglers will also suffer other limitations, such as in casting and the control and playing of quality fish. It is important to analyse your own performance and style and improve upon your techniques to overcome any deficiency or bad habits.

What then are the basic guidelines and points to consider when choosing a rod.

**Float Rods**
Apart from obvious characteristics such as lightness and balance, the main considerations must relate to the line strength to be used and the range and type of fishing. The 'traditional' match rod has a fine spliced tip action which is designed for rapid line pick-up on the strike, coupled with shock absorption qualities to help prevent 'cracking off' at the hook length when using one pound and 12 oz bottoms. These rods are ideal for trotting on flowing water when fishing with tight line to a stick float or avon, but many top anglers find them a little too 'fast' for waggler fishing at long range on flowing or still waters, especially if a larger species of fish is expected. The preference

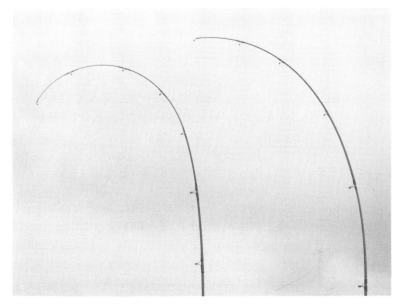

*Fig. 1. Rod tips, spliced and straight taper.*

then is for a rod with a slower taper tip, which is still 'tip' actioned but is also more progressive through the tip to the middle section, spreading the action further down the rod. This also has the advantage of giving the angler more 'feel' through the rod, and of course the extended action does cushion the lunges of the fighting fish much more, essential when playing larger fish. The problem is that a thicker tip increases the risk of breaking on the strike, but by carefully analysing the ring spacings on the top section, and in some cases by splicing in a softer material, the 'speed' of the tip can be slowed down, cushioning the force of the strike. I have both types of float rod and find that for the majority of my fishing I seldom use the really fast spliced tip. Having said that, a number of anglers I know seldom use anything else. Again, individual style and preference are the final deciding factors.

One thing we are all agreed upon is the importance of buying the best quality. This may not necessarily mean the most expensive, but the more you pay the better the quality of the materials and design. Admittedly a good angler can catch fish on anything, but when the chips are down reliability and performance must be taken for granted, leaving the angler free to concentrate on getting and hitting bites and successfully landing fish.

**Leger Rods**

This area of match fishing has seen the most dramatic changes over the last 20 years or so. Once the Cinderella of angling and looked down upon by most anglers as a last resort, legering in its now many and varied forms is 'the' method of amassing high weights, and most river and lake match records are held by users of leger tactics. Because of the many different legering methods, a much larger range of rods is needed to fish effectively if you intend to be an all round matchman, fishing both still waters and rivers. Whilst the development of the swing tip was the great breakthrough for still water legering, the swim feeder has had the biggest impact on the match fishing scene in the last few years, and it is this area which has seen the most dramatic developments in the design of specialist rods.

For feeder fishing in flowing water from the upper and middle reaches of the river down to the tidal stretches, at least three different types of rod design are needed to cope with most of the conditions likely to be encountered. The types I carry are an all carbon quiver tip rod which can be used at 10′ or 11½′, an 11′ heavy carbon feeder rod with a spliced-in fibreglass top piece, and for the tidal stretches and flood conditions, a very stiff 11½′ carbon 'big pig' rod capable of punching out up to 4 oz + feeders. In addition to these, a lightweight quiver tip and a wand are also needed for closer range legering. Except for the wand, which has a mellow, progressive through action, the rods

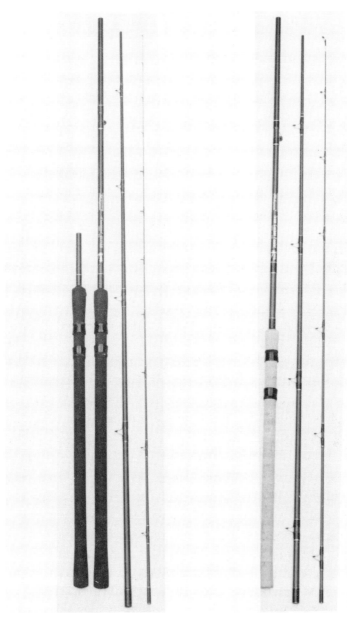

*Fig. 2. Feeder rods.*

used for legering in flowing water have their action in the top and middle sections. These rods have to perform two contradictory functions. They must be strong enough to punch out heavy feeders, and at the same time be sensitive enough to indicate bites and play large fish on fine hook lengths. When considering the rods used for long range and heavy flows, this balance is even harder to achieve. These rods do not have quiver tips, as the pressure of the flow against the line, even when fished upright, would render a quiver tip useless. Indication is registered directly on the rod tip.

Rods for fishing still water have totally different qualities. They are shorter, 9 – 10′ being the usual length, and with a smooth, progressive tip to through action to cope with the striking and playing of large fish on small hooks and fine bottoms. This is one area where I consider hollow fibreglass still reigns supreme for rod construction. When considering a modern replacement for my old 9½′ glass swing tip rod, I was unable to find a carbon rod which could improve upon the qualities of the old rod apart from it being lighter. As the rod is always placed on rod rests whilst fishing, this was the least important consideration. Finally I settled for a rod constructed from a blend of graphite and hollow fibreglass, thus retaining the classic soft through action with a limited weight saving in the butt section. I have been very pleased with the performance of this rod, but still use my old faithful as a back-up, or for light feeder work on still water.

For fishing at club level, one float rod and two leger rods will cope with most average situations, and as you will be fishing against opposition with similar armoury, you will seldom be struggling except in the most extreme situations. As you will have gathered, anyone considering competing at open level on both still and flowing water is looking at a considerable invest-ment on rods alone, and we have not yet discussed the pole.

*Fig. 3. Radial wand and tips.*

If you are very lucky and have a reasonable idea of the qualities you require of the various types of rods available, and have the help and guidance of a qualified mentor and are prepared to shop around until you find what suits you, then only the one outlay will be needed. But often it is a case of trial and error, and this can result in expensive mistakes, especially if you are tempted into taking advantage of the 'bargain offers' you see advertised in the angling press. These are generally products which dealers are unable to sell, either because they are badly designed and do not do the job they are supposed to do effectively, or they are a discontinued line which has been superseded by an improved model. In both instances it means that something superior is available, and it is this you should be considering.

**The Pole**
This is another aspect of angling which has seen an amazing

increase in both popularity and product development, but also where mistakes in initial investment can prove to be the most costly of all. Fortunately, if the suggested guidelines are followed, even the most inexperienced angler can sort the wheat from the chaff. The minimum length of pole should not be less than 11 metres, and should only weigh around 1 kilo (35 ozs) or less. When fully extended it should have very little sag at the tip, certainly no more than about 6″ at 11 metres. This is a true test of stiffness. The sections should slide on and off easily and smoothly.

If you know what you are looking for and follow the above guidelines, this is one area where you can take advantage of secondhand bargains. Several hundred pounds can be saved in this way, as top class poles can cost well over £500 when new.

Shorter, budget priced poles should only be considered if you intend to fish only at club level, or for use as training aids if you are uncertain as to whether you will take to using pole methods. It must be stressed that to succeed at open level you must learn to master a long pole in a variety of situations and conditions. These will be dealt with in the chapter on pole fishing.

**Reels**

As with the choice of rods, reliability and performance is linked to price and quality. It is also important to balance your equipment, and this can only be done by ensuring that you match your rod and reel combinations from the same relative part of the range. Only two types of reel need to be considered – the fixed spool and the closed face. The latest fixed spool reels available from well known tackle companies such as Shakespeare, can be relied upon for quality in design and performance, and this, coupled to an efficient after-sales service, offers excellent value for money. Modern features such as carbonite skirted spools, rear drag adjustment, automatic bale arm opening systems, high ratio retrieve, match capacity spools, and dual function automatic or manual bale arm return, are all now common features built in to increase efficiency and to save valuable seconds on each cast and retrieve. For most float fishing and legering tactics these are the matchman's main work horse, but there are many occasions when it pays to also have a closed face reel available. Though there is not such a varied range of these reels, due to their simplicity, they are ideal for trotting in flowing water or when fishing in a strong facing or side wind, as there is no bale arm or exposed spool for the line to get blown around or tangled. When trotting on flowing water, engaging the pick-up after striking and hooking a fish is a simple and smooth operation, and most designs have overcome the old problem of the line 'bedding' in on the narrow spool causing it to stick or snatch on the next cast or trot.

Care and maintenance of your reels should always be your top priority. Never allow them to rattle around unprotected in your box or basket. Always keep them in waterproof reel cases. After each outing make sure they are dried, and clean off any accumulations of mud or ground bait. Most top matchmen return them to the manufacturer each close season for servicing and inspection. In this way they are confident they will not be let down at a critical moment. If possible try to stick to one make and model, thus saving on duplication of line strengths, as all spare spools will fit any reel; also if a reel should fail when fishing it can be quickly replaced without breaking down the tackle.

**Line and Hooks**
The choice of line and hooks as with the choice of float rods, is down to personal preference within the guidelines of design and performance. No two brands are exactly the same, and the individual must arrive through trial, error, and experience, at

a combination which suits his style and application. Even so, there are certain basic points which must be considered before a proper evaluation of the various types available can be made.

As there are hundreds of different patterns and types of hooks, it is important to simplify the range we use, and to consider the factors which should govern the choice of hook type and size.

The type of hook to be used is mainly dependent on the choice of bait and the size of fish we are likely to catch. For fishing with maggot for small fish up to one pound in weight, a fine wire crystal bend hook would be the natural choice. For fishing with casters, punched bread or small worms, a fine wire round bend hook is the type to use. Both these patterns are lightweight and have the minimum effect on the natural buoyancy of the bait. When fishing with small hooks for large fish such as bream and chub, a hook of the same pattern bend with respect to bait type is used, but the wire is of the forged variety for added strength, and the point is often offset to left or right, which is known as reversed or kirbed. Most match patterns are reversed.

The disadvantage of the forged pattern is that the increased weight of the thicker, stronger wire can affect the presentation of the bait. Sometimes this means we may be forced to compromise and sacrifice hook strength for bait presentation in order to get bites. Provided we are aware of the limitations of hook strength, and the area of water we are fishing is relatively snag free, then big fish can be successfully played and landed on 'unsuitable' tackle. The object is of course to get bites, but this must also be balanced by the risk of losing good fish on hooks that are too fine or small for the task. Ten bites produced by using small hooks which as a consequence result in eight lost fish and only two in the net, is obviously not as good as only four bites on properly balanced tackle which results in three or four fish in the net. These points will be examined in more detail in later chapters.

Regarding the question of hook size, the deciding factor is the size and type of bait. For fishing with maggot and caster baits, fine wire hooks in both round and crystal bend patterns, sizes 16, 18, 20 and 22 should always be carried. Size 24 in a crystal or round bend pattern may also be needed for fishing with single pinkie, squatt, or bloodworm. A range of forged reverse hooks with a crystal bend in sizes 20 – 16 for maggot fishing, and with round bends sizes 18 – 12 for fishing caster, worm and bread will also be required. Larger forged hooks with a round or crystal bend in sizes 10, 8 and 6 should also be carried if large baits such as luncheon meat and sweet corn are likely to be used. Most modern hooks are chemically sharpened with smaller, neater, barbs. The points on the finer hooks are very fine and prone to being easily blunted or curled. A regular check of their condition must be made, and the hook should be changed at the slightest sign of bluntness.

## Line

With so many brands and types of line now on the market, the knowledgeable angler can fish more effectively than ever before, but for the inexperienced, as with other items of tackle, too wide a choice can create more problems than it solves. The important point to remember is that different lines have different qualities, and if these can be identified and applied you will be able to cope with a variety of conditions and situations. The most important difference between certain lines is their ability or otherwise to float, and their elasticity or lack of it.

Regarding the ability of a line to float, this can be an advantage or a disadvantage, depending on the type of fishing. If float fishing with a waggler or antenna float at long range, especially in still water, a line which can be pulled under the surface easily should be used. If you are using a stick float, or in some cases a waggler on flowing water in an upstream wind situation and you wish to slow down the bait, the line is deliberately left on the surface. It must also be left on the surface in calm conditions when trotting the far bank of a river, to allow the angler to 'mend' the bow which is bound to form in the length of line lying of the surface of the faster water in the middle of the river.

All line will float when new unless some action is taken on the part of the angler to sink it. The difference between brands is that some lines are more difficult to sink than others. In some cases it may only be the surface tension which holds the line on the surface. In others it could be due to a higher buoyancy factor in the line itself. The surface tension problem can be overcome by overcasting, placing the rod tip under the surface and giving a couple of fast turns with the reel to bring the tackle back to the baited area. The surface tension holding up the line will then be broken. When a line is new it should be run through a cloth soaked with washing-up liquid. This will help to make it sink more easily. I treat all my long range leger and float fishing lines in this way. The line I use for trotting is always untreated, and I use a buoyant, high stretch line for this type of fishing.

The second point to consider is elasticity. Standard European monofilament lines all have a reasonable degree of stretch built into them, although some are more elastic than others. These lines also tend to be thicker, more abrasion resistant, and to have a high knot strength. There are now a number of different brands on the market which have totally different qualities to the standard monofilament lines. These are the 'super strength' lines. They offer a higher breaking strain for a given line diameter and are made from pre-stretched monofilament or copolyamide type materials. They have very little elasticity, are less durable and more easily damaged, and unless properly tied, have a much lower knot strength or knot holding ability. Unaware of these disadvantages, many anglers bought them when they first came out, because the obvious advantage of the lower line diameter meant they could fish stronger or finer hook lengths. They then became very disillusioned when they experienced a higher percentage of lost fish due to 'cracking off' on the strike, knot failure, or lack of 'feel' when the line was approaching breaking point. They then dismissed them and returned to their tried and tested brands of traditional line. What these anglers failed to realise was that it is not a replacement for standard monofilament lines, but if you are prepared to alter your approach to overcome its limitations and utilise its advantages, it does play an important part in overcoming certain problems. I have found that the lower breaking strains are ideal for pole fishing when used in conjunction with an elastic shock absorber. The lack of stretch is countered by the elastic, and full benefit can be taken of the higher breaking strain or lower line thickness as required by the conditions. When using a rod and reel, it is best used in combination with standard monofilaments. At long range when legering or float fishing, it makes an ideal main line, the low stretch helping to pick up the line and connect with the fish more quickly. The hook lengths should still be made of standard mono. The use of it for hook lengths should only be considered in conjunction with standard main lines and at times when the fish are being extra line shy and you cannot produce the goods on standard mono. Provided knots are tied very carefully and the strike smoothed out to counter the lower resistance to shock absorption, it will produce bites and in turn fish which may not otherwise have been forthcoming.

## Accessories

Most anglers contemplating match fishing will have most of the accessories normally needed to fish efficiently, but a few points may be worth considering.

**Bank Sticks and Rod Rests**
Under normal conditions the standard aluminium tubular bank sticks are more than adequate for setting up rod rests and keep nets. There are times, however, when good quality telescopic bank sticks capable of being extended to 8' or 9' may be necessary. These are essential on occasions when the banks are unsuitable or too hard to secure a bank stick and the bed of the lake or river has to be used. They are also necessary when legering in fast flowing water where the rod needs to be supported in an upright position (see Fig. 4).

*Fig. 4. Feeder rod on rod rest in upright position.*

Rod rest heads also need to be adequate. For float fishing the head needs to be broad so that the rod can be placed on to it without having to look down. For legering, the type developed by the late Freddie Foster, which uses a completely snag free circle of polythene tubing, helps to prevent the line snagging and being broken on the strike, a common occurrence with flat top rests, especially in windy conditions (see Fig. 5).

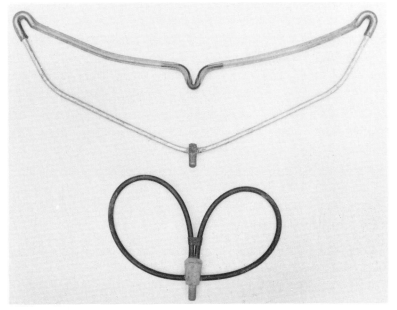

*Fig. 5. Rod rest heads. Large flat and round leger type.*

## Catapults and Throwing Sticks

When feeding at medium range, a throwing stick is far more efficient at keeping the bait in a tight circle than hand throwing, but catapults of various sizes and strengths are needed for feeding loose bait or ground bait at long range. It is essential to carry spare elastics and ties for each one so that quick bank side repairs can be carried out if one should fail during a match. This point is often overlooked by many anglers, and many potential match winning chances have been lost due to catapult failure. For loose feeding, small pouches are superior to the plastic cups which are more suitable for ground baiting. Surgical rubber is now more widely used in preference to the traditional square catapult elastic and is less liable to abrasion and breakage. Most systems allow the replacement of either type.

## Tackle Boxes

The most important feature to consider in any tackle box is accessibility. A well laid out box with every item readily available is essential for a fast turn round when tackle changes become necessary during the course of a match. Some top anglers have tackle boxes which look like disaster areas, and find this no handicap. Others have boxes which look as though they are laid out for Royal inspection, with everything neat and tidy and in its place. Most anglers strike a balance between the two extremes. The important thing is to be able to immediately locate whatever is required and to be able to see at a glance any reduction or losses in essential items of equipment, preferably before rather than during a match.

## Bait Aprons

For years I managed quite comfortably without a bait apron, considering the cost to be money which could be better spent on more essential equipment. Eventually I received one as a gift and have since wondered how I previously managed without one. Over the course of a season it has saved hours in turn round time, especially when feeder fishing or float fishing in a standing position. The important consideration is to ensure that it has at least two bait compartments and that they are the full width of the apron and of adequate depth. A number of smaller pockets for holding small items of replacement tackle, hook disgorgers, etc, are also essential features.

I hope that, having read this chapter, you are more enlightened rather than increasingly confused, as to the amount and type of equipment you may need to compete successfully. Some anglers may consider that a helicopter will be a necessary item to transport the volume of tackle they could acquire. This is, of course, another important consideration. One current fashion, especially with those match anglers who use the pole regularly, is to carry their own portable platform, thus ensuring a stable, comfortable, and efficient lay-out regardless of the condition of the bank side, when they eventually reach their peg. The obvious problem is getting to the peg with your equipment, especially if you draw a long walk, with enough energy and time left to set it up and perform as efficiently as your equipment will allow. When fishing local waters where normally you can be certain beforehand of the exact amount and type of equipment required, this is less of a problem. The real difficulty is in assessing your probable requirements for a club or open match at a distant venue which is relatively unknown to you, or which has a number of variable sections all requiring a different approach. Instead of being able to rationalise your equipment, more likely than not you will be tempted to take everything but the proverbial kitchen sink. Murphy's law more or less guarantees that if you do leave anything at home you will draw a peg where it will be needed. There is also the added problem of being spoilt for choice as to method or bait.

Normally these situations affect the newcomer to the match fishing scene far more than the old hand, who will have had much more experience of the variety of waters around the country, and most important of all, will have access to the match regulars' 'grapevine'. This will provide an up-to-date breakdown of the current form and condition of a venue, thus allowing him to take a limited amount of tackle, bait, etc, and to use a more single-minded approach. The moral of this increasingly complex chain of probabilities is that 'If you can't take a joke, don't join', because match fishing will expose you to an unimaginable number of frustrations and disappointments before you begin to reap the rewards of success.

# 2   BAITS

The variety of baits which can be successfully used in angling is endless, but for the match angler, only the few types covered in this chapter need to be considered in all but the most rare of situations or conditions. Everyone dreams of discovering an unknown secret formula or additive, and cleaning up with it. But it will always be a pipe dream, and no aspiring match angler can afford to divert precious time and energy away from the real essentials, which are the correct preparation, feeding, and presentation of the bait to the fish, having regard to the prevailing conditions. Recent seasons have seen the adoption of a wide variety of additives and attractors by match anglers at all levels in the sport. In many cases certain of these do seem to be effective on occasions, and these will be discussed later in this chapter. The important point to remember is that no matter how effective some of these may seem to be in capable hands, they can never be a substitute for ability.

**Maggot baits**
These have been and will continue to be the mainstay of match anglers in this country. Whilst other baits, on their day, can out perform the maggot or caster, they cannot be collected or produce as consistently or in sufficient quantity and at a price the tackle trade and the average angler could consider acceptable. Neither is their use as simple and straightforward or as reliable. The quality of the average commercial maggot is now at its peak, and provided they are properly prepared prior to use, they can be used with confidence. New dyes are now being developed and marketed, and the variety of colours available is also greater than ever before. Maggots can be bought

already dyed, or if preferred you can buy natural white maggots and colour your own. Final pre-match preparation of your bait is the same whether you buy commercial coloured maggots, colour your own, or even breed your own hook baits. The object is to remove all grease and odour from the skin. This is best achieved by riddling off any old sawdust or meal and putting the maggots into a large unsealed plastic container along with a good helping of fresh maize meal. This can be obtained from most good corn merchants or pet shops. They should be left in a cool, dry place and at no time should a lid be placed on the container. Provided everything is kept dry the bait cannot climb out. Be wary of using metal trays or containers. A rapid drop in air temperature overnight can cause condensation on the sides of these, resulting in the maggots escaping. Pinkies are especially good at this, and only need a hint of dampness to start them performing. Several changes of meal may be needed before the bait is thoroughly cleaned. Any attractors can be added just prior to travelling to the match, after riddling the bait for a final time and adding enough fresh meal to prevent the bait from sweating.

**Pinkies**

These are the larva of the green bottle fly, and are much smaller than the ordinary commercial hook maggot. They are very useful for feeding a swim without over feeding the fish, especially in cold weather or in a canal fishing situation. The general theory is that if you feed with pinkies, the fish you have attracted will see the larger maggot you are using as your hook bait and be overcome with greed and fight to get at the larger sample. One some occasions this method works, but on many others it is not successful. If you are feeding pinkies and fishing a large maggot on the hook, especially when the fish are on the small side, they will become pre-occupied with the pinkies and ignore the larger maggot, or just suck it at the end. In these circumstances it pays to scale down your hook size to a 22 or 24 and to fish with a single or double pinkie as your hook bait. In adverse conditions when the fish are not feeding freely, using the pinkie as a hook bait can get you extra bites. I never go match fishing without a supply of pinkies, especially in the winter months when I often use more pinkies than any other type of maggot. Pinkies can be kept longer than other types of maggot before turning into a chrysalis. This is an obvious advantage in keeping down costs, as any unused bait can be refrigerated and used on another occasion. The disadvantage is that unless your local dealer has a regular turnover of fresh pinkies, the bait can be old when you get it, and whilst this may be acceptable for feeding, the pinkies will be too small and tough for use as hook bait. The feed streak in a fresh pinkie is much less pronounced than it is in a normal maggot, and this makes identification of its freshness all the more difficult.

**Squatts**
These are a very small, frail maggot, and are very difficult to keep in good condition especially in hot weather. They are best stored in damp, fine red sand, as they are when supplied from the tackle shop. Unlike other maggots they are never sold neat. A pint of squatts will always contain a large proportion of sand, and this must be borne in mind when ordering a specific quantity for a match. Despite these disadvantages they are essential when maggot fishing at a bream venue, especially during the summer months. They sink very slowly and due to their softness and relatively inert state, large quantities can be mixed in easily with ground bait. As the ground bait breaks up as it falls through the water, it leaves behind a slowly sinking cloud of squatts which is very attractive to bream, which will be induced to feed if present in the swim. When you cast your hook bait into the

baited area, the fish will have no difficulty in picking it out in this cloud of tiny squatts. When mixing your ground bait, a small fine mesh riddle must be used on the bank side to separate the squatts from the sand. Those squatts not required for immediate use must be left in the damp sand.

## Casters

Although at many top match venues the great caster revolution of the 'seventies has given way to the maggot renaissance of the 'eighties, there are still many waters and occasions where the fish will respond to casters, and on these occasions they are undoubtedly a matching winning bait. Most good tackle shops can now supply good quality casters in reasonable quantities, though often you will have to order them well in advance to be certain of your supply. If you do not have the benefit of a good shop in your area, or if supplies may be hit and miss in quantity as well as quality, you will need to know how to turn your own.

During the summer months, maggots laid down the week-end before the casters are needed should turn with sufficient speed and in sufficient quantity. The problem of timing becomes much greater during colder weather. Often during the winter maggots may need to be laid down two weeks before you need them to enable them to turn in time. Another point to consider is the quantity of bait needed. If you need to be certain of two pints of casters, four pints of maggots need to be laid down. As you can see, although the cost of shop bought casters may be twice that of maggots, turning your own for purely economic reasons is a non-starter, as you need twice the number of maggots to ensure you get sufficient casters on the day. The only time you benefit is if you use casters on a regular rather than an occasional basis, and you regularly practise in mid-week. Then you will use the casters you have turned from the surplus bait after the match of the previous week-end, and this will make the whole operation a little more cost-effective.

When laying down maggots for turning they must be in a large open container and put into a cool place. Clean, damp, sawdust is the best medium in which to keep them, as this helps reduce the natural dehydration of the maggots as they turn.

When a maggot first changes into a chrysalis it slows down its movements and starts to contract. The skin then goes through a very rapid series of colour changes. A white maggot would begin to turn light yellow, then orange, through red and to dark red, then to almost black. At the same time as these colour changes are taking place the metabolism of the maggot is also changing. One of the side effects of this changing process is the effect upon the buoyancy of the chrysalis. If allowed to go too far it will float. It is very important that the chrysalis is caught at the right stage of the changing process and the process slowed down, so that when the bait is used it will sink.

The only way you can slow down the process is to reduce the temperature and the amount of air. The point at which you do this is between when the chrysalis is light yellow and before it becomes dark orange in colour. If the chrysalis is allowed to get to the dark red stage it will be too late as the bait will then float.

There are several ways of separating the bait at this point: one is to pick the casters off by hand as they turn, at intervals of a couple of hours, or if a large quantity is required, to run the maggots through a 3 mm mesh. The live maggots will wriggle through the mesh leaving the casters and any dead maggots on the top of the riddle. It is very important to remove any dead maggots from the casters at this stage as they rapidly decompose and will sour the bait if left.

The casters are then put into a plastic bag and stored in a cool place, preferably in a refrigerator. If you do store them in a refrigerator, do not put them in the freezer compartment as this will kill them. Although they are no longer wriggling they are still very much alive. Do not keep them in the bag for more than a day without opening the bag to allow more air into it. You need to reduce the amount of air they receive but not completely starve them of it. Never keep casters in water – this is the biggest cause of sour casters. They will drown and start to decompose inside their shells. When you are actually fishing with them, especially in the summer, you can put some water in the bait tin to stop them turning, as they will be used immediately.

Casters should always be used within a couple of days from starting to turn. Sometimes when turning your own casters they may start to turn on the Wednesday as you will be using them on the Sunday. In these circumstances they must not be kept in a plastic bag or they will die and turn black. They should be kept in a bait tin with the air holes covered with cling film.

After the first couple of days when you have turned say ¾ pint of casters, take them out of the plastic bag and put them in a small 1 pint capacity bait tin or margarine tub. Then put cling film over the top of the container and fit on the lid. This will stop any air getting into the container but at the same time leave some air inside to keep the casters alive. You then store the container in a cool place or refrigerator. In this way they will keep for 4 – 5 days.

When you buy casters from the tackle shop they will be supplied in plastic bags and should be fresh. Certainly they should not be more than one day old. When you get them home, put them in a bait container and fit over the cling film. In this way they will keep much fresher than if left in the plastic bag. Avoid any shop bought casters which look 'burned' where the casters are touching the side of the bag, which means they are several days old and are probably dead. Never buy casters which have been kept in water. A lot of dealers still keep their casters in this way due to ignorance of the fact that casters die in water. Never subject your maggots to a lot of heat if you want good casters. Always keep them in a cool place and allow them to turn naturally. Forced casters are small and shrivelled looking, and no good at all. In the winter you may have to bring them into the house to get them to turn in time for when you need them, but always leave them in the coolest place possible.

When fishing with casters the hook is buried inside the caster. If you are getting bites and the caster is being nipped off at the end and you are not connecting with the fish, try fixing the caster to the hook in the same way as you would hook a maggot. A fine wire round bend hook with a medium to long shank is the best type to use. If you ask your dealer for caster hooks he should know the type you require. When using double caster it is important to hook them at alternate ends. This will help to reduce the tendency for the bait to spin on the retrieve and kink your hook length (see Fig. 6).

On the day of the match you can keep the casters you are

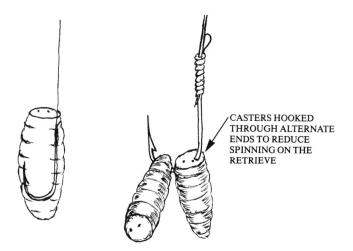

CASTERS HOOKED THROUGH ALTERNATE ENDS TO REDUCE SPINNING ON THE RETRIEVE

*Fig. 6. Correctly hooking casters.*

using in water, once you have reached your peg. It is important to skim off any floating casters at this stage. Do not throw these away as they can be used as hook baits. The natural buoyancy of these floaters will help to counteract the weight of the hook, helping the hook bait to act as naturally as the loose feed you are using.

Some top anglers prefer all their casters to be of a similar colour so that they all sink at the same rate. This could be an important consideration on occasions when fishing flowing water, when the darker, slower sinking casters could take your fish downstream and out of your swim. But for still or slow moving water, mixed colours are preferable as they help to spread out the fall of the bait, making your regular feeding a more constant trickle of falling samples. This also has the effect of bringing the fish up in the water and closer to the source of the feed, which in turn will speed up your catch rate.

## Hempseed

Many match anglers consider hempseed to be the number one attractor, especially for roach fishing, and very few will go to a match without taking hempseed in one form or another. Its properties of holding fish in the swim are indisputable, and most coarse species are attracted to it.

Either whole seeds, or ground hemp mixed into groundbait are used in conjunction with caster or maggot, but it is far more effective when used with casters. On those occasions that fish can be caught whilst using hempseed as the hookbait, considerable catches can be made, but it seldom performs during a match for reasons best known to the fish, although it still works well as an attractor.

When loose feeding hemp it is important to realise that it sinks much faster than casters or maggots, so its introduction must be made much further down the swim on flowing water. Always feed hemp separately from casters or maggots unless using groundbait or a swimfeeder.

Always pre-soak the seeds for about 24 hours before cooking them. This helps to swell the seeds and reduce the time it takes them to split. Many anglers add a non-toxic dye to the hemp to alter the colour of the white kernel, red being the most popular colour.

After straining the hemp, the water used to cook it in can be kept and used to mix your groundbait if you intend to use any.

### Gozzers

For as long as match fishing has existed, and probably well before that time, the breeding of superior hook maggots to the commercially available bait has been undertaken by dedicated anglers, many of whom have perfected it to a fine art. There is no doubt in my mind that the gozzer, properly prepared and presented, does give you an edge, especially when bream fishing. They are lighter and softer than commercial maggots and generally smaller, although some anglers are capable of producing absolute monsters. I have found that it is the nature of the maggot as opposed to its size that is important. Because it is lighter it sinks more slowly, an obvious benefit when fishing on the drop, and once on the bottom it lifts more easily against the weight of the hook when sucked up by a feeding fish. By studying the feeding habits of coarse fish in a tank, it will be observed that fish very rarely pick up a bait directly off the bottom. Instead they suck the bait up, rather like a vacuum cleaner. As a fish moves over a carpet of loose feed, any baits which do not rise up and into its mouth are normally ignored. It follows that a maggot which is prevented from lifting in a natural manner due to the weight of a hook and the stiffness of a heavy line, will in most cases be ignored by the fish. Using a more buoyant bait such as a gozzer or a floating caster will therefore give you a better chance. Once a fish has picked up the bait, it often blows it in and out several times before taking it back to its pharyngeal teeth to chew. Due to the softness of the gozzer it will be more readily accepted by the fish and will be less likely to be blown out again, giving a much better chance of hooking the fish.

How do we produce gozzers? The first requirement is some form of meat on to which the fly will blow and the maggots will feed. Normally sheep or pig hearts, chicken portions, or pigeons are the most popular mediums. It is then necessary to ensure that only the gozzer fly blows the meat. Fortunately a characteristic peculiar to the gozzer fly is that it will only lay its eggs in dark or very dull places. The meat should be put into a biscuit tin or similar container with a couple of inches of fresh bran covering

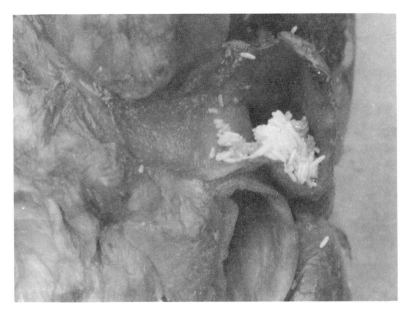

*Fig. 7. Fly blow in heart artery.*

the bottom. Slits are cut in the meat and opened up and the meat is laid on top of the bran. If a whole pigeon is used the beak is kept open with a piece of match stick as the fly normally lays the eggs in the pigeon's throat. It is not necessary to pluck the pigeon. If hearts are used the fly usually blows in the opening of the artery (see Fig. 7).

The tin is then placed in a dark corner of a shed or garage and the window or door left slightly open. Another method is to place the tin outside under a dustbin lid which is held up by a brick. The lid should be left on top of the tin so that only a small gap large enough for the fly to enter is left. During warm, dry weather, you should get a blow on the first or second day. In cold, wet weather it may take two or three days to get a blow. Weather conditions not only affect the time taken to get a blow but also the hatching and growth rate of the maggots. In warm weather, the whole process from first putting down the meat to the maggots reaching full size takes only 6 – 7 days, but during a damp, cold spell it could take from 10 to 14 days. As the bait needs to be used within one or two days of reaching full size, timing can be a problem. If you intend to ensure you have a regular supply of gozzers for both week-end match days and mid-week practise sessions, by organising yourself and regularly putting down meat every Sunday and Wednesday during the summer and autumn months, you should always have fresh, fully developed gozzers on match days regardless of the vagaries of the climate. By having regular bait breeding taking place, the flies will tend to hang around the area, thereby speeding up the time taken to get a blow. Never throw unused bait away. By scattering a few of the gozzer casters in the corner of the shed or garage, fresh breeding stock will hatch at regular intervals. This may sound a rather smelly and anti-social occupation which requires understanding neighbours and wives, but in fact, provided the rules are followed, no problems should arise.

Once the meat has been blown it should be wrapped in newspaper. A large paper about six pages thick is usually sufficient. Keep the sheets together as opposed to wrapping the meat in layers of separate sheets. This makes inspection and colouring of the bait during the development period much easier. The parcel is laid on the layer of bran inside the tin and the lid tightly closed. Air holes are needed in the lid but these should not be too large or rogue flies will lay their eggs through the holes. After about 3 days the parcel should be opened and the contents inspected. Provided weather conditions are favourable the maggots should be about half grown and feeding well. This is the time to put in any colouring if you intend to colour feed the bait, and extra meat if you think the feeding maggots will need it. If colouring powder is to be used this can be sprinkled dry into the meat, as the juices caused by the feeding maggots will activate the dye. If annatto is used the roll must be cut up and melted in hot water to form a yellow paste and the paste applied to the meat with a brush. The parcel is then rewrapped, placed back in the tin and covered with fresh bran. When the maggots have reached full size they will finish feeding, leave the remains of the meat, and work their way through the paper and into the bran. When this happens the contents of the tin should be tipped on to a wire mesh riddle, allowing the maggots to fall out of the old bran and meat and into a container containing fresh bran or maize meal. The remains of the meat should be put in a plastic bag and sealed to prevent any smell escaping, and either burned or put in the dustbin. Once the bait has cleaned itself in the fresh bran or maize meal, it should be put in a small container into which is added some fresh damp bran, and placed in a cool place or refrigerator. The reason for the damp bran is to prevent excessive dehydration of the gozzers, which not only makes them smaller but also tougher. Any flavouring or additive can be added to the bait at this time.

This procedure sounds very complicated, but the only difficult thing about it is convincing yourself you can do it successfully. Once you have tried and found how easy it is, there will be no stopping you in the future.

*Fig. 8. Bloodworm scraper.*

## Bloodworm and Jokers

These are the larvae of the gnat and midge. Although they are now becoming increasingly available in some top class tackle shops, the only reliable supply is by collecting your own. Before you can do this you need to locate waters where they can be found in reliable quantities. The bloodworm is only found in still waters. Most still waters contain bloodworms, but those with slight pollution and little or no fish in them to eat the bloodworms are normally the most productive. Ponds which are about $3' - 4'$ deep and with a silt bottom are the most productive. The equipment required to collect them is a pair of chest waders, a specially adapted tray or bucket, and a scraper blade which has been made to fit a landing net handle (see Fig. 8). By wading through the pond and pulling the scraper through and just below the surface of the silt with a smooth sweeping action, the bloodworms are picked up on the edge of the blade. When the blade is lifted out of the water after each sweep, the larvae along with other debris, can be scraped into the container with your finger. Inside the container is a wire mesh tray. The bloodworm wriggle through the mesh into the lower part of the container, leaving most of the debris on the mesh. This can be lifted out and washed off at regular intervals.

Jokers are found in streams, and again slight pollution and silt bottoms are the features to be looked for. Areas below sewage outfalls are often quite prolific. Again a scraper can be used, but if the bottom is weedy the silt can be disturbed with a stick and the jokers caught in a fine mesh net as they float upwards. The are best stored in damp, fine peat, wrapped in small flat newspaper parcels and placed in a cool place or refrigerator. When damp they can be safely stored for several days.

**Worms**
Worms have been used as bait since angling first began in prehistoric times, but it is amazing how many anglers do not know the correct way to put a worm on a hook. Much of the attraction of a worm to the fish is in its wriggle. Why then do anglers do their best to prevent the bait from carrying out this most important of functions? By looping it round and hooking it several times they prevent the worm wriggling. By hooking it through the saddle where all the essential organs of the worm are located it will quickly die and stop wriggling. So how do you get the best from your worm? A worm should always be hooked through the head. The hook point should be inserted just below

the tip and come out again just above the saddle (see Fig. 9). If hooked in this way it can wriggle freely and will last in the water for a considerable time. The main reason anglers fasten a hook through a worm several times is to stop the bait flying off the hook when they cast, but by doing this they are preventing the worm from acting as an attractor. If you are fishing at a long distance, the worm can be kept securely on the hook with either a caster or a maggot on the hook after fixing on the worm. In the case of a large hook, a piece of bread flake or crust can be pressed on to the point to hold the worm on the cast, and if not required it can be 'struck off' once the bait has landed in the water.

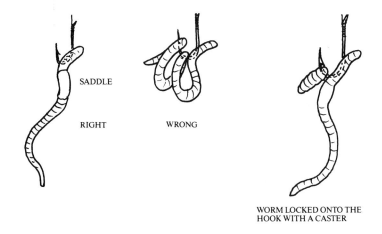

*Fig. 9. Correctly hooking a worm.*

Worms come in two sizes. The small red worm and brandling worms, and the mighty lob worm. The red worms and brandlings are ideal for general fishing for bream, tench, small perch and roach. The lob worms are used for chub, barbel, perch and carp.

Red worms and brandlings are fished on hooks from size 16 to 10. The lob worms from sizes 8 to 2. They can be float fished, legered, or freelined, and consequently are a very versatile bait. They can be fished singly or in bunches, or head or tail only can be used.

Locating worms is also fairly easy provided there are no drought conditions prevailing. Red worms or brandlings can be found underneath compost or manure heaps. Lob worms are found either in the soil or on the surface of lawns at night. The worms found on lawns are usually the largest and juiciest. Any mown grass area will have worms. Parks, garden lawns or grass verges on estates will have some, but some areas will be better than others. When you first go worm hunting it may take some time to find the most prolific areas. Once these are located, only a few minutes work will be needed to replenish your stock. The way to collect them is to go out after dark when the grass is damp or wet with dew. Take a flash lamp with a shaded beam, and a bucket. Tread gently as any vibration will cause the worms to shoot back down their holes. The worms will be lying half in, half out of their holes, stretched out on top of the grass. When you pick one up in your torch beam do not try to grab it in your fingers as it will just contract and shoot down the hole. Look for the darkest part which is the head, then press hard down with your finger on the lightest end away from the head. The worm will contract, but will not be able to get passed your finger. You then take hold of the head and gently ease it out of the hole. Do not pull hard or you will end up with only half a worm, which will quickly die.

Keeping worms can be difficult, particularly lob worms which are very difficult to keep alive, especially in bait tins. To keep lob worms in good condition for any length of time you must have a fairly large container such as a bath or large bowl placed in a cool shady place and half filled with good quality soil with several inches of grass cuttings on the top. This must be kept well watered but not too wet.

Keeping red worms or brandlings is easier. Damp peat in a bait container is all that is needed, but if you want to toughen them, damp moss is more useful. By turning the tin over each day the worms will keep working down through the moss. This will produce very tough muscular worms with plenty of wriggle. Do not allow the peat or moss to dry out and make sure the air holes are clear.

### Bread Baits
Whilst they can give exceptional results when pleasure fishing, bread baits have a very limited use in match fishing situations, but on the occasions when they are successful, good weights can be expected.

### Bread Flake and Paste
A very good alternative bait when the usual range of small baits are ineffective, especially in waters which hold larger fish such as bream, carp, chub, tench, large roach and rudd. Often when fishing venues which hold larger fish it is advisable to open the proceedings in a match with these baits as opposed to using them as a last resort when other baits fail. An odd chub or carp can be taken early before the swim is disturbed by constant casting and, hopefully, by the playing and landing of fish. Disturbance of the swim will often put the big fish down, but by pursuing them at the outset if they are present, you stand a much better chance of catching them, and of putting several pounds of fish into the net in the first half hour of the match. Obviously knowledge and experience of the water are essential in these circumstances.

### The Bread Punch
I consider this to be an essential item of tackle, especially for

fishing in still waters such as ponds, lakes and canals during the summer months. It is normally made of aluminium with a selection of brass heads which screw into the end and are stored inside the body when not in use. It allows you to put a tiny pellet of slightly compressed bread on to a small hook such as a size 16 or 18. This swells in the water covering the hook completely and making a soft, attractive bait. Always use medium or thick sliced bread as the thin does not compress sufficiently. Place the slice on a hard surface such as a tackle box lid, and press the punch into the bread. This cuts the bread, leaving a small pellet inside the head of the punch. Next insert the hook point, remove the pellet from the head, and gently position it around the bend of the hook. It is then ready to be cast.

Always use fresh bread. Never take more than half a slice out of the bag at any one time or it will go dry before it is all used. Used slices which have gone dry can be mashed with water in a bait container and small pieces can be flicked in around the float to attract fish into the swim. In sunny conditions try to keep all the bait in the shade so that it will last all day. This is one of the cheapest but most effective methods of fishing.

Although the use of a bread punch is generally associated with summer months and high water temperatures, it can be very effective for winter fishing in canals, often attracting a better class of roach and bream. Multi-head punches are now available for punching out large numbers of pellets for use as loose feed. To ensure that these sink, the bread should be dampened and pressed overnight. When punched as you need them the pellets are heavier and easier to throw out, and will always sink. The hook bait can still be cut out of a fresh slice.

### Ground Bait
The last five years have seen a radical change in the development and use of ground bait in match fishing. This has been largely

influenced by a greater understanding of the continental use of additives, attractors and techniques, and of course by the development and use of the swim feeder. Prior to this period of enlightenment, the only effective method of introducing large quantities of bait samples such as squatts and casters at any sort of range, was by containing them in heavy balls of ground bait. This was fine on waters which contained huge shoals of bream and other large fish which would consume these vast quantities of food, but as fish stocks declined and match venues came under increasing angling pressure, the introduction of ground bait in traditional quantities became the kiss of death. Now that bait samples can be introduced at long range by using a block end swim feeder, the use of ground bait is much more considered. The cereal content of ground bait is also much less, due to a better knowledge of alternative ingredients, and these days the words 'ground bait' are associated more with the method rather than with the bread crumb, which was the previous main ingredient.

Many continental ground baits are now available, each containing the personal recipes of various successful continental anglers. Additives such as ground hemp and peanuts, dried pigeon droppings, and a variety of oils and spices, are some of the ingredients used. By using combinations of these special mixes with our traditional varieties of cereal ground baits, the properties of the mix can be adjusted to suit various conditions. The cereal content which dictates the food value of the mix can be cut and replaced by various sands, soils and clays, which give different advantages and properties which in turn can control how the mix behaves during the throwing, sinking, and breaking-up periods.

To try to explain all the various combinations which could be used would take up the whole of this book and be very confusing. I therefore propose to cover some of the properties of the various ingredients, and by understanding these you can experiment using buckets, bowls, tanks or actual fishing situations, until you arrive at your own successful combinations and have a full understanding of how they work.

### Coarse White Bread Crumb
Very seldom used alone in any quantity. Small proportions are good for use as a binder on fast flowing water, or to provide floating attractors in mixes, or when used in conjunction with a bread punch.

### Fine White or Brown Ground Bait
Can be mixed with ground rice, or 'Explosif', a French cloud ground bait, to provide a cloud attractor when surface fishing or fishing in shallow water.

### Slicer Crumb
Brown, light-weight, coarse flaky crumbs, the by-product of bread slicing machines. Main ingredient when you require a high cereal content in your ground bait. Helps to keep it light and fluffy and provides floating particles in the ground bait cloud.

### China Clay and Soil
Used as a cereal substitute when you do not want to overfeed the fish. When mixed dry with other ingredients before wetting, the dried clay will not congeal and will form a good cloud effect in the water. The soil adds bulk, and light or heavy soils can be experimented with to vary the rate of fall through the water.

### Silver Sand
Gives added weight to the ground bait and helps to break it up more quickly.

**Powdered Ground Cork**
Makes a good cloud effect when mixed with fine crumb to bind it.

**Sieved Leaf Mould and Peat**
A light medium which will just hold together when dampened, and break up to form a dark slow sinking cloud when it hits the surface. Normally used in conjunction with blood worms.

Ground sunflower seeds, hemp seed, pumpkin seeds and peanuts all make good attractors for various species; as do flavourings such as crushed trout pellets, molasses juice or meal, vanilla, cinnamon, dried blood and a vast range of other spices and sweeteners; all of which are available at most good tackle shops or food stores.

Various safe non-toxic dyes can also be bought in tackle shops, of which red is the most popular.

These are some of the most common ingredients used in ground bait.

Ground baiting tactics are discussed in the chapter on pole fishing, and the chapter devoted to general feeding methods and tactics.

# 3  FLOAT FISHING

Many aspiring match anglers, myself included, in the early stages of learning the ropes have put a high degree of priority into the buying or making of a large collection of floats to cover every possible variation in conditions likely to be encountered in this country. In retrospect, I sometimes think that too much knowledge can have a negative influence. If anything we should rationalise the variety of float patterns we carry, using just a few basic types, and put much more thought into varying the shotting patterns. I could illustrate, as many of you possibly could, twenty different types of floats and dozens of shotting combinations to suit all the various situations that are likely to be encountered, but that would only be duplicating advice already available in dozens of other books and articles. What I want to do in this chapter is expand your train of thought rather than the contents of your float box. It is not that I consider shotting diagrams to be either unnecessary or unimportant – far from it, I shall be using many illustrations myself – but I hope that you will look at them in a completely different light.

The main object of float fishing is to use the float together with shots or weights, to present the bait to the fish in a manner that is natural and acceptable to them in the prevailing conditions, and to indicate through the float that the bait has been taken. By altering the position or size of a shot, or by changing the size or type of float, we can alter the presentation of the bait or the way in which a bite is indicated. One of the most difficult problems is to convince people that the modern trend of having nearly all the weight around the float when fishing still or slow moving water, and having only a couple of dust shots down the line, can in many cases be counter productive. Many anglers accept the fact that they must use an olivette to concentrate the weight down the line when using a pole, and where they also have the benefit of direct rod tip control over the tackle. But they cannot relate to having weight down the line whilst float fishing with a rod and reel where they have a lot less rod tip control and where under certain conditions it is more necessary.

In deeper water when bites are coming from on or near the bottom it results in lost time, in windy conditions in loss of stability, and in slow moving drains or canals subjected to surface drift, either a completely wrong presentation of the bait or the giving of wrong information as to the rate or direction of the flow. A correctly shotted float can give many more indications to the angler than just the fact that he has a bite. It can tell him the nature of the bottom and of any variations in depth or in the rate and direction of any flow or undertow not being shown on the surface. It can also show whether the bait has settled or if it has been held up or intercepted by weed or fish on the way down. Most importantly it shows the exact position of the bait at any time, an obvious point but one that is often taken for granted and not utilised to its full advantage.

A couple of small shots down the line are all that is needed for taking fish on the drop near the surface and mid-water areas, or for bottom fishing in shallow water in fairly calm conditions, but more weight must be considered in most other circumstances. I must emphasise the word 'considered'. It is amazing how many anglers shot up floats out of habit rather than with regard to the prevailing conditions and situations, and having done so make little or not adjustment to shotting and depth during the rest of the session. What these anglers are doing is waiting for the fish to come to their bait instead of taking the bait to the fish, or keeping in touch with the fish as conditions change. Let me give you an example.

You are fishing about 4 rod lengths out in a lake. It is 8′ deep, fairly calm, and the main species are skimmers and roach. The sun is shining and you start by using a 3 AAA waggler with a fine sensitive insert. You shot up using the pattern shown in Fig. 10A.

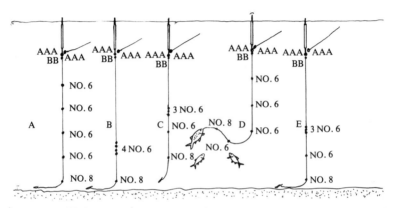

*Fig. 10. Altering shotting in stillwater.*

This would be the normal starting set-up as you wish to establish just where in the water the fish may be feeding. You would begin by loose feeding maggots or casters on a little and often basis. You would never leave the bait in the water any longer than a minute between casts during this opening period. After 10 minutes you get your first bite. This comes from a bottom feeding fish well after your tackle has settled. Casting in again you get another bite, again after your bait has reached the bottom. At this stage you have established that the fish are feeding on the bottom. Now you must increase the catch rate by saving some of the time it takes for your bait to reach the fish. This would be achieved by moving the top 3 No. 6's to join the lower one, as in Fig. 10B. Several more fish are taken in quick succession, then you get a bite whilst the bait is still falling. After this the bites stop. The chances are that the fish have moved up in the water. The first thing to do is to move three of the four No. 6's back up the line to just below the mid-way point and bring the bait up off the bottom by lowering the float a foot (Fig. 10C). Bites start again, but instead of the indication being by the float going under, increasingly the indication of a bite is by the delay in the falling shots acting on the float tip as the fish intercept the falling bait and just hold it up.

We continue to lighten and shorten off to keep in touch with the fish (Fig. 10D). Eventually bites tail off and only odd bites are now coming from near the bottom. As the bite rate is now slow and we want to know if the odd fish can still be taken in mid-water as well as on the bottom, we compromise with our shotting pattern and revert to pattern E, which is the same as C but is laying on, instead of being off, the bottom.

The falling off in bites has also coincided with a freshening of the wind, and the initial calm conditions have been replaced by a choppy surface and the tackle is starting to drift with the wind. In this situation a change of float to one carrying more shot is needed. Provided a silicon fast change float adaptor is being used, this will not take long. A float of the same pattern or with the addition of a body can be used which has a capacity of, say, 2.SSG. This is a one-third increase on the original size of 3 AAA. The same shotting pattern can be used but instead of 3 No. 6's being bunched together we now use 3 BB's. One of these is the one which was under the AAA locking shot, plus 2 BB shots from our box. One of the number 6 shots removed can be used to 'back shot' and help to sink the line, and a number 4 is added under the locking shot to 'trim the float' (see Fig. 11A). This should help keep the float stable and indicate whether any 'undertow' is developing, by the tackle moving against the direction of the wind.

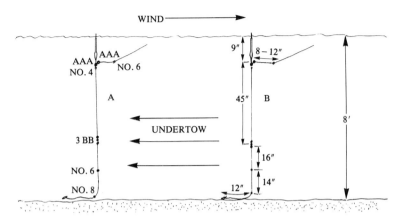

*Fig. 11. Shotting in windy conditions.*

In extreme conditions it may be necessary to put all the shot down the line.

This is best achieved by fishing a sliding float. Any type of waggler or antenna float can be used as a slider. Special sliding floats with small pin-hole size rings can be a great handicap. Due to the small ring the line is slowed down and takes too much time to pull through. Often it can stick and needs to be tweeked to make it move again, causing a jerky fall of the bait. Also if a large float needs to be used the strike can be impaired by the float being pulled through the water. The solution is to use a float with a standard sized ring and to fit a small balsa bead with a pin hole through the middle on the line between the float and the stop knot (see Fig. 12). This will slide freely up and down the line and the large ring on the float will allow the line to run smoothly and freely, as both the tackle sinks through the water, and also on the strike. These beads are easily made by cutting 3 mm long pieces from 4 mm balsa dowel. A pin is pushed through the centre of the bead which is then dipped into varnish. When the varnish is dry the pin is removed leaving a small diameter hole (see Fig. 13).

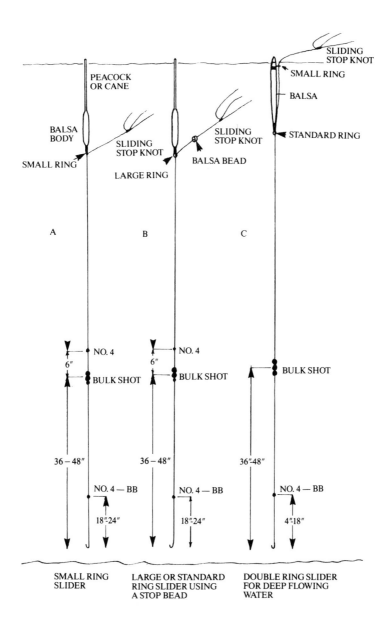

*Fig. 12. Sliding floats.*

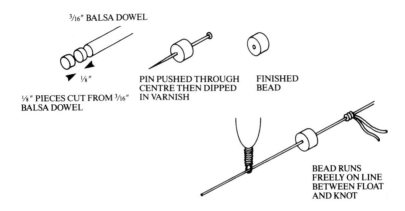

*Fig. 13. Making a stop bead for sliders.*

As well as also being used in deep water, sliding floats are also useful for overcoming situations where you are pegged in a swim that has a great deal of bankside growth, or other obstructions restricting normal overhead casting methods. Sliders are always cast out using a smooth under-arm or side cast, casting into the wind if tangles are to be avoided.

### The Sliding Stop Knot

It is important to learn this very simple but very versatile knot. Apart from its use as a stop knot when using sliding floats, it can also be used to make an adjustable link when link legering. This allows the leger angler to adjust his length of tail very quickly by moving the link up or down the main line.

The knot is formed by taking a separate piece of line approximately 6″ in length and normally of a higher breaking strain than the line you are using. This is then doubled over and laid along the reel line (see Fig. 14). One loose end is then taken and wrapped around the main line four or five times. The end is pushed through the loop you made when you first doubled the line over and the two ends are then pulled tight. The tighter you pull the more it will grip the line.

You are now left with your stop knot and the ends are about 3″ long. The natural thing to do would be to trim these ends neatly off, but it is important that this is NOT done. The ends should be left long to stop them catching in your rings when you cast. This would have a serious effect on your casting distance.

If an adjustable leger link is required, a longer length of line is needed to make the knot. After the knot has been tied, the lower end can be trimmed off leaving the one long length on to which you would tie your bomb (see Fig. 15).

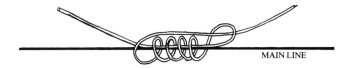

*Fig. 14. Sliding stop knot.*

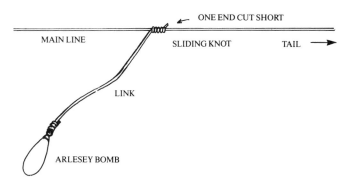

*Fig. 15. Adjustable leger link.*

Provided you fully understand the reasons behind these various changes of shotting, experience gained by putting these principles into practice will help you to analyse a situation as it develops, and to adjust your terminal tackle accordingly. At all times you must try to imagine what is happening under the water and put yourself into the position of the fish. You also have to work out what is happening to your loose feed. Sometimes bites stop because your loose feed is not going where you think it is, and by casting around, the re-appearance of bites in an unexpected direction or area can give you a clue as to water movement that is not being indicated by your tackle, but which must be taking place under the surface. Under-tow is a prime example. Sometimes things go the other way. You throw in your feed to counter the undertow, only to discover that the surface drift is pulling it so far the other way that by the time it reaches the bottom, the two directional forces have cancelled each other out. In flowing water, surface speed and bottom current can vary considerably, making it difficult to establish what is happening to both tackle and bait. We will look at these points in greater depth later on.

A number of important points about the positioning of the bulk shot and indicating shots also need to be considered. Except when using a slider, the bulk shot must always be positioned below the half-way point, so that the rest of the tackle cannot 'pivot' on this point and 'back tangle' with the locking shots on the cast. The indicating shots must also be positioned at slightly unequal distances to prevent tangles around the bulk shots. In an 8′ deep swim, the following distances shown in Figure 11B should explain this more clearly. The easiest way to check, especially as we will be moving shots around during the session, is to pivot the hook on the No. 8 shot, and make sure it cannot reach the No. 6. Then pivot the No. 8 shot on the No. 6 ensuring it does not reach the bulk BB's. We must then pivot the whole terminal tackle on the bulk shot, ensuring the hook is below the locking shots. This is also the method of checking the positioning of your shots when using a strung out pattern with a stick float. Observing the above guidelines in the positioning of shots will help to reduce tangling on the cast, but tangles will still occur unless you can master the art of 'feathering' your line. This is achieved by slowing the rate at which the line is coming off the spool with your finger, just prior to the tackle hitting the surface of the water. By doing this the terminal tackle is straightened out, eliminating tangles completely and allowing the bait to fall through the water in an even line, ready to indicate a bite at any time. It is essential to learn how to achieve this. Tangles cost time, and time is precious in a match. Also the steady feeding and casting rhythm you have worked yourself into will be broken, and this can be disastrous when fish are coming regularly. When you first try to feather your line you will probably be a bit clumsy and cause the line to snatch or jerk the tackle. Do not be put off if this happens. Keep practising and the correct feel will soon be developed, and you will find you will soon do it naturally and unconsciously as you progress.

One float I use in still water under certain conditions is a 'special' which I make up myself by adapting commercial wire stem stick floats (see Fig. 16B). Half a cocktail stick or a reversed piece of fine crow quill is fitted into the tip, and the float is fitted onto the line with double rubbers. Micro dust shot are spaced in shirt button style down the line, and the whole rig is fished with as much as 2 ' or 3 ' of line lying on the bottom. In windy conditions it is always cast into the wind and downstream of the undertow (see Fig. 16A). A No. 6 or No. 8 back shot is needed to sink the line between the float and the rod tip, unless you need to use the wind on the line to hold position, as is sometimes necessary when the undertow is extremely strong. What you are effectively doing is 'laying on' against the undertow, and I am often the only person getting bites under these conditions by using this peculiar method. It can also be used in canals or drains with a very slight flow, as well as in still water under calm conditions. The secret is to fish well over depth, feathering the tackle on the cast to ensure everything is fully straightened out. Always shot the tip down as fine as conditions will allow.

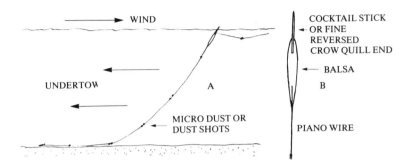

*Fig. 16. Laying on with a wire stem stick float in still water.*

I have now covered the main types of float patterns used on still and slow moving water. Always use a float big enough to reach the area you intend to fish comfortably, so that if the fish move further out you can follow them without losing time in changing and reshotting your float. A large float properly shotted is just as sensitive as a smaller float with the same size of insert or tip. The sensitivity of a float is dependent upon the cross-sectional area and length of tip showing. The type of material used does not matter. The only way to make a thick tip more sensitive when fishing at long range is to use one of the new hollow tip floats. As water can fill the centre of the float tip it is sensitive to the low total cross-sectional area of the tube wall only, whilst still giving the high degree of visibility offered by the large diameter (see Fig. 17).

The only slight disadvantage of this system is that in calm conditions a bubble can sometimes form in the cut-out, preventing the water from flowing into the tube and interfering with the setting of the tip. A slight twitch will clear it easily, but a bite taking place whilst the tackle is falling will not be registered by the usual delay in the shots acting on the float tip. This

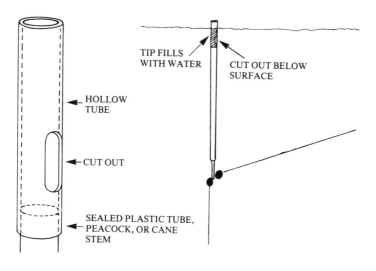

*Fig. 17. Hollow tip float.*

problem does not occur quite so much in choppy water.

The last few seasons have seen the introduction of carbonite tube and clear plastic tube as float making materials. One system uses interchangeable tips of different lengths and thicknesses, including sight bulbs, making a set of 5 or 6 floats capable of a large number of variations to suit changing conditions, without changing the basic float. This is an important time saver, and I have found these floats to be sensitive and reliable, with very accurate shotting guides printed on the float stem.

We have looked at ways of using weight to overcome some of the problems associated with fishing still water. Let us now look at float fishing in flowing water. Here the main considerations are the direction and strength of the flow in relation to the direction and strength of the wind, the range at which we intend to fish, and the speed of our tackle in relation to the speed of the current.

## Waggler Fishing

If the flow is slow and steady and the water not too deep, then unless the surface area is being affected by strong wind, the rate of flow will be fairly even from top to bottom. In these conditions a straight insert waggler or antenna float fished bottom only at the speed of the current, will perform quite adequately, and the same shotting patterns already discussed will be sufficient. The important thing to consider in selecting the type of shotting pattern is the length of the swim and the rate of fall of the loose feed or groundbait. You will always need to try to simulate this. If you are able to use ground bait, then the feed will be getting to the fish much quicker than if you were using just loose feed, so a concentrated shotting pattern would be used to get the hook bait down to the fish just as quickly. If the flow is light and you are loose feeding, a slower sinking pattern would be chosen so that the hook bait will sink through the water with the loose feed. These considerations will be looked at in greater detail in the chapter on feeding methods.

Because a waggler is normally fished 'loose', i.e. after casting, the tackle is allowed to go through the swim unchecked, it is important where you cast the tackle. If cast slightly upstream too great a bow will be formed in the line by the faster water in the centre of the river, especially if fishing the slower flow on the far bank. This will make connection with any bites extremely difficult. To minimise this you should always cast slightly downstream, mending the line to the float as soon as the tackle hits the water, then letting it run through unhindered. When striking with a waggler at long range you must always strike with a smooth sideways sweep into the near bank with the rod pointing downsteam. In this way you will strike down the bow of your line. Try striking upstream and you will have to pull the bow against the flow, losing the power of the strike due to the cushioning effect of the water (see Fig. 18).

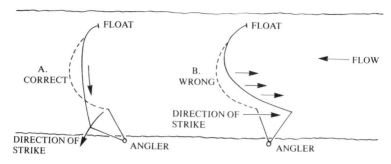

*Fig. 18. Striking with a waggler at long range on rivers.*

For fishing in faster water the floats are made of straight peacock quill or of peacock quill with balsa bodies. Some of the floats covered earlier in the still water section are ideal for this type of fishing. These would be the larger ones without the fine inserts, as these can be a handicap when fishing bottom only on fast flowing water. The method is often used with a small shot or the hook length dragging on the bottom providing it is snag free (see Fig. 19). You need a thick tip to counter the drag without it going under. The only occasion where a tip with a sensitive insert would be used is in waters with a very light flow, where the fish will have more time to take the bait and may just hold it up. In this case a finer insert will register a lift bite better than a thick tip.

The wagglers with the balsa bodies are normally used for long range fishing in slow moving waters. The reason you sometimes need such large floats using as much as two swan shot locking the float to the line is to give enough weight to cast the distance required.

When using heavy floats like this it is important to use a heavier main line to prevent breakage.

When fishing in faster flowing waters with the hook length or a small shot dragging the bottom, you need as much as 1″ of float tip showing above the surface. The tip will move up and down as the tackle goes through the swim, dragging the shot along the bottom. As soon as the bait is intercepted by a fish the float will dip sharply under.

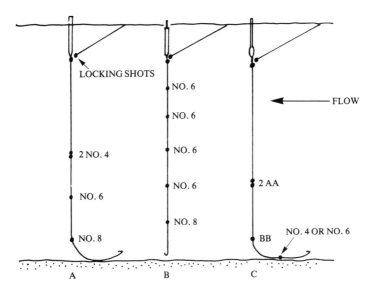

*Fig. 19. Shotting a waggler for flowing water.*

In windy conditions the float will be either held up or pushed through too quickly, depending on whether the wind is upstream or downsteam, so in both these cases more weight will have to be put down the line to stabilise the float and to give the flow something to pull on (see Fig. 19C). Sometimes when the wind is upstream and the fish want the bait slightly slower than the flow, this can be achieved by leaving the line on the surface and by lifting the line into the wind with the rod top. To hold the bait back in 'downstream' wind conditions you need plenty of weight down the line to hang on to. By using a waggler with a thick top and under-shotting it so that an inch or more is showing, it is possible with practise to hold back, gently lowering the float with an even pull and feeling it down the swim. Once this method has been mastered and you can competently distinguish between real bites and false bites caused by your own actions, this can be a really deadly method and give you an edge over the stick float anglers who will not be able to control their tackle in a downstream wind situation. Having said that, do

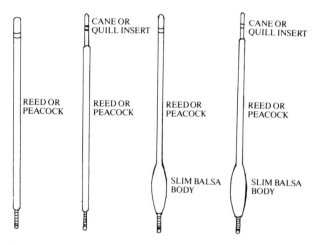

*Fig. 20. Wagglers.*

not become pre-occupied with fishing the bait at normal or reduced speed. It can often pay to let the wind bow the line in a downstreamer and pull the tackle through faster than the speed of the current. Why this sometimes works I do not know. What I do know is that when bites are not forthcoming by using traditional and 'sensible' methods, you should keep an open mind and try anything, no matter how silly it seems.

On faster flows and in deeper water, the speed of the current can often vary considerably at different levels. In some cases where the bottom is uneven and contains large rocks and other obstacles, it can even come back the other way; in other words the water is running in both directions at the same time. This can also happen in some man-made drains that are controlled by sluice gates or lock gates, or in the tidal reaches of rivers. Often these changes can be detected by reading the float as it goes through the swim, but to achieve this you must have weight down the line for the differences in flow to act upon.

## Stick Floats

In many textbooks you see diagrams of the traditional stick float pattern of equally spaced shot, increasing slightly in size as they get nearer to the float. This is fine if you are fishing in shallow or slow moving water and are taking fish on the drop. In deeper and faster moving swims, most of the shot must be below the half-way point, for several reasons. First of all it is important to get the bait down to the fish and under control as soon as possible, and also to have the feel of the tackle in the area where you are fishing, which is near the bottom. Looking at Fig. 21, you will see that I have indicated by using arrows, the difference in the rate of flow between the surface and the bottom of the river. By concentrating the shotting at various points in the lower half we can work the tackle through at the rate of the lower flow where our feed and the fish will be concentrated.

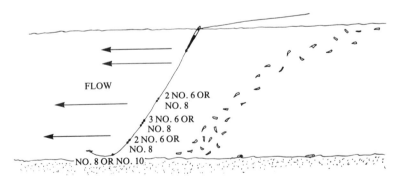

*Fig. 21. Different rates of flow.*

Note also the way in which the feed falls through the water. It will travel down the swim much further as it falls through the faster surface and mid-water flow than through the lower third of the water. Note also the grouping of the shots at points A, B and C in Fig. 22.

As the tackle falls through the water, or when the tackle is checked as it moves down the swim, the way it reacts to the water around it can be varied by altering the groupings from these points, downwards or upwards. If the fish want the bait hard onto or near the bottom, the grouping shown in Fig. 21 will do the job. As the fish move into the swim they may start to come up in the water to intercept the loose feed, and you may need to shorten your depth, or a slower fall or higher lift of the hook length when checked may be needed. In this case one or two shots can be moved from point B to point A, and one shot from point C moved up to point B (see Fig. 22A). If the bait is being taken and this is not being indicated through the float, the No. 8 at point D can be moved closer to the hook, and the two shots at point C spaced out to new positions. The other groups can be moved slightly up or down to keep the spacing right and prevent tangling on the cast (see Fig. 22B).

Note that in all cases a BB shot is positioned directly under the float. This is there to keep the float stable and to prevent too much lift of the float when the tackle is checked or held back, and also to aid casting. The shot sizes shown can be stepped up or down using 6's, 4's, BB's or dust shot combinations, depending on the rate of flow and the size of float. The important thing to remember is to use groupings of shots to vary the presentation at any time throughout the session. If you should find that the fish want the tackle held back and presented slower than the flow, the float will need to be over-shotted slightly to prevent it from riding too far out of the water. Ideally the tip should be just visible above the surface. The rate at which the tackle is either held back or allowed to run through with the flow can be controlled in several ways.

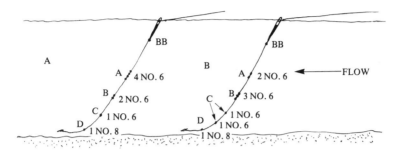

*Fig. 22. Shotting a stick float.*

If the float and tackle is only to be slowed down very slightly, the drag caused by the line being pulled off of the spool combined with the friction of the rod rings can often achieve this for you. Often not realising this, some anglers think they are trotting through at the speed of the flow, but due to these effects upon the line they are not.

A common method used to control the speed of the tackle is by feeding the line off of the reel with the fingers, but this is very difficult to achieve smoothly without jerking the float and the tackle. The most efficient method is to use rod tip control.

The tackle is cast in and the line mended to the float. The rod tip is then moved smoothly upstream, allowing the line to pull off of the spool. The line is then trapped with the finger against the spool and the rod tip is moved downstream with the tackle at the speed you require the tackle to be put through the swim.

A considerable distance can be covered down the length of the swim before the rod needs to be moved back upstream and more line released from the spool, repeating the process as often as is necessary to cover the length of the swim. Each release takes only a second to be achieved, and this is the only time that you are not in full control of the tackle.

Often when using this method the bite is felt simultaneously with the float indication, and a smooth tightening of the line is all that is needed to connect with the fish. Stick floats do, of course, have their limitations. Direction and strength of wind can aid or limit the range and controllability of the tackle. A slight downstream breeze can be overcome to some extent by using a back shot and by keeping the line under the surface, but it is impossible to hold hard back without pulling the tackle into the nearside bank. This is true of all floats fixed to the line both top and bottom. A strong upstream wind, instead of being helpful, can sometimes ruin presentation when the fish want the bait put through at the speed of the flow. This is a particular problem on rivers such as the Bristol Avon which run from east to west. In many parts this river is very deep and slow moving, so to get the bait to move with the flow and against the prevailing south westerly wind is quite a problem. A favourite method is to use a traditional crow quill Avon float. The body of the float helps the current to act on the float, aided by the concentrated shotting pattern, and the tip of the float is fine and sensitive, to indicate the slightest bite (see Fig. 23). The concentrated weight

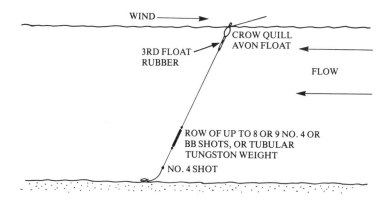

*Fig. 23. Shotting an Avon.*

is made up by stringing BB's or No. 4 shots in a long bunch, or by using the new tungsten tubular weight, which is very efficient and less prone to tangles than large groups of split shot. When using a crow quill float, a third rubber halfway up the lower steam is essential to stop the float from snapping due to the tendency for the stem to double up when striking. In fact it is good practice to use a third rubber on all 'double rubber floats, then if the line should cut through the top rubber, as can often happen, the float can still be secured properly by moving the spare rubber into place. A great time saver.

### Balsa Trotting Floats

In very deep powerful flows, floats capable of carrying weight up to a total of 4 or 5 swan shot may be needed. This brings us to the range of balsa floats. Because of the strong flow it is essential to get the bait down to the fish as quickly as possible. An example of various combinations of shotting is shown in Fig. 24.

The pattern of float I prefer in the balsa range for fishing with small baits is the shouldered balsa or pacemaker. It can be fished running through with the flow, and when checked the shoulder helps to prevent the float from riding too far out of the water. Under favourable conditions it can also be used effectively holding back. The thick topped balsa floats are used mainly with big baits or when fishing at long range. These are situations rarely experienced in match fishing where mostly small baits are used and the length of peg is normally limited. Even so it may be handy to have at least one for those rare occasions when the conditions are so bad that you may be using a big bait such as worm or flake, in the hope of connecting with a match winning 'dog', or have one or two empty pegs below you.

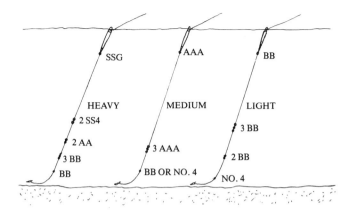

*Fig. 24. Shotting balsa trotting floats.*

## Laying On and Float Legering

On many occasions when fishing flowing waters in conditions of low water temperature and/or times of flood, the fish may be reluctant to take a bait trotted through in the normal way and will only take a static bait. In these conditions laying on or float legering can be a very effective way of getting bites. In slow or steady flowing water, this can be easily achieved by moving the float up a foot or two overdepth, and the bulk shots up by the same amount, leaving a couple of feet of line lying on the river bed. Notice that I said you move the bulk shots up the line as well as the float. It is important to have these shots clear of the bottom if this set-up is to work efficiently (see Fig. 25). This point is often overlooked by anglers who, after a period of trotting without results, resort to laying on tactics but only move the float up the line and ignore the terminal tackle. In many cases the addition of extra shot immediately below the float, or down the line with the bulk shot, is also required. This is to prevent the float from riding too high in the water and increase the sensitivity of the tackle.

Normally when laying on, the tackle is cast downstream and

then held back in the current, allowing the tackle to straighten out and swing in towards the bank. The rod is normally held straight out from the bank and supported by a rod rest. The distance from the bank at which the tackle lies is normally governed by the length of rod protruding out over the water. Bites can often be induced by occasionally lifting the rod and allowing the tackle to inch itself downstream, covering a greater amount of the swim than if the tackle is left in one position all the time. In this way it is possible to find 'hot spots' in the swim where the fish are lying. This may be due to an obstruction such as weed or rocks, or perhaps a shallow depression in the river bed, all of which provide shelter for the fish from the main flow. These cannot be seen by the angler from the bank, but by searching the length of the swim in this way they can be found by the sudden appearance of bites that only occur in these particular areas.

When fishing smooth flows, by undershotting a straight peacock waggler it is possible to lay on with the float connected by the bottom end only. This can be a very sensitive method, but you cannot inch the float down the swim as you can with a float that is connected by the top and bottom. If you wish to move the bait, you must cast the tackle well down the swim and inch the bait back up the swim towards you.

The advantage of laying on to legering is that the position of the bait can be easily pinpointed by the position of the float. The bait can be accurately placed over the hot spots much more easily than when legering.

When fishing fast or strong flowing water, laying on with float and shots becomes impractical because of the large amounts of fixed lead that need to be attached to the line to get the bait down to the fish and to set the float. The fish need to move all of this to indicate a bite and can feel the resistance caused by all this weight against the current. In these conditions legering methods need to be employed, but we can still keep the advantage gained by using a float to indicate the position of the bait in the swim as well as indicating the bite. This method is called float legering.

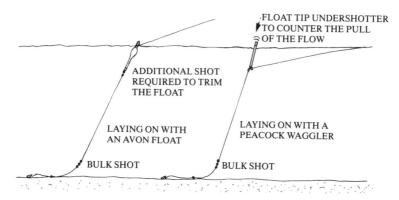

Fig. 25. *Laying on in flowing water.*

A small feeder or a small Arlesey bomb can be fixed on the line and allowed to slide up and down the line freely. A leger stop or split shot can be fixed above the hook length giving the required length of 'tail' (see Fig. 26). Some split shot may still be needed to set the float tip to the required sensitivity, but the bulk of the weight will be in the leger, and it is important to set the depth accurately when using this method, taking into account the angle of the line. The weight will be on the bottom and the tip of the float just above the surface. By adjusting the angle of the rod tip to the float tip, small discrepancies in this distance can be counteracted (see Fig. 27). Only trial and error will teach you this. When using this method larger baits may sometimes be very effective. Many match anglers will argue that when conditions are adverse, the tackle and bait size should be scaled down rather than up. But for general fishing I have often found the opposite to be the case. A large bunch of maggots, a worm, or a piece of bread flake will often produce a more positive bite on this kind of rig than a small bait fished on a small hook.

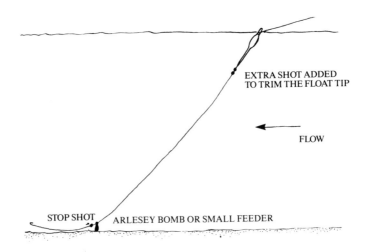

EXTRA SHOT ADDED
TO TRIM THE FLOAT TIP

FLOW

STOP SHOT   ARLESEY BOMB OR SMALL FEEDER

*Fig. 26. Float legering in flowing water.*

The best type of float to use when laying on or float legering in flowing water is the Avon type. The top buoyancy built into this design of float is essential if stability is to be achieved. The size of the float used is of course dependent upon the depth and strength of flow.

Float legering on still water is not so commonly used these days due to the great advances over the last few years in bite indicators. Even so I think the method is worth covering as some anglers do get more pleasure from watching a float than a swing or quivertip, and on some waters it may be more practical to use float legering methods to overcome certain localised problems. When float legering in still waters, the type of terminal tackle used is the same as when legering with a swing or quiver tip. A float of the antenna type is connected to the line above the tackle

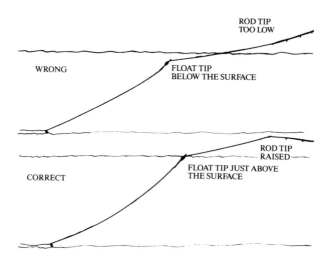

*Fig. 27. Adjusting the line angle with the rod tip.*

and is allowed to run freely up and down the line. It is stopped at the required setting by using the sliding stop knot described in the section covering sliding floats. The distance between the terminal tackle and the float will be greater than the depth of the water (see Fig. 28), and has to be set by trial and error. A rough guide to help with this setting would be to start at 1½ times the depth of the water, although the distance from the bank at which we are fishing will be a contributory factor in deciding the position of the knot. The rod is placed on the rod rest after casting, and the final setting is done with the reel by adjusting the tightness of the line. In waters that have a deep layer of either weed or mud on the bottom, this is a very good way of legering. Instead of having the hook length or tail longer than the bomb link which is normal when legering, the link is made much longer and the hook length is fixed paternoster style, allowing the bait to hang above the bottom (see Fig. 29).

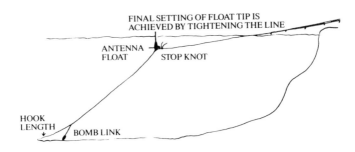

*Fig. 28. Float legering in still water.*

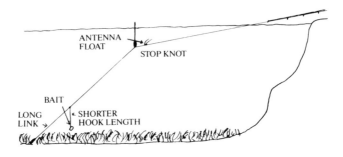

*Fig. 29. Paternoster rig for float legering.*

## Lead Free Shots and Weights

I do not intend to discuss the rights or wrongs in the swan/lead debate. The fact is that legislation has been imposed which must be adhered to. On the positive side it has led to the development of alternative types of weights as well as materials, some of which may be of benefit to the match angler, such as the tubular weights already mentioned. Many anglers will now use groups of No. 8 shots in place of single No. 6's or No. 4's. Some may consider this to be an unwelcome compromise, but many others will find it will have a long term advantage as it enables them to shuffle shots about and will give them more precise control over the action of the terminal tackle.

Of all the substitutes now available, I feel that for both practical and traditional reasons those that look and work like the old lead split shot will be the mainstay of the match angler. Provided care is used, I have found these to be easier to open and close, and far more durable than lead. I have always filed a secondary 'v' in my shot with a small file to make it easier to open them with my thumb nail when I want to change or reposition them whilst fishing, and this works equally well with the substitutes. The important thing is not to chew or trim your thumb nails, as these are some of your most essential pieces of equipment. When using AAA or SSG sizes of the new shots I have found that by using the tiny plastic or silicon pole float sleeves now widely available, you can counter any possibility of the harder material damaging your line, and can make positional adjustments more easily and with confidence. It also reduces the tendency of these larger sizes to slip, especially when being used as locking shots (see Fig. 30). The only real fault with them at the time of writing is that they tend to be very shiny, and this could be a problem in very clear or shallow water due to the flash of reflected light frightening the fish. Some people have said that the shine can be dulled by soaking in vinegar, but I have tried this, and if anything it makes them even brighter. After all, vinegar has been used for years to de-oxidise gold and coins rather than to dull them. Constant exposure to air and water does dull them in time, but I have found that a light spraying with a matt black paint aerosol does give a reasonably durable dull finish, which probably has a greater effect on my confidence than perhaps it does on the fish, but confidence is always an important consideration, so it is well worth the effort.

The new shots do tend to be larger in proportion to the old lead equivalents but they still maintain the same ratio of approximate sizes, i.e. 2 AAA = 1 Swan: 2 BB = 1 AAA: 2 No. 4 = 1 BB, and 2 No. 6 = 1 No. 4, etc. It is essential to understand and remember these ratios to save valuable time when setting up or changing the float type and size during the course of a match.

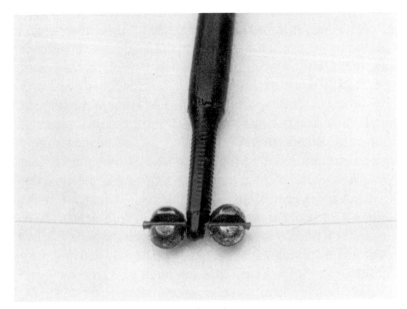

*Fig. 30. Large shots being clamped on sleeves.*

## Float Construction and Materials

Unlike when I started fishing, the range and quality of commercial floats is tremendous. Many anglers still prefer to make many of their own floats, but more for pleasure than necessity. Having said that, I am going to discuss the construction of some of the most essential patterns, as it is important to understand how and why these combinations of materials come about.

When choosing or designing a float a number of considerations must be taken into account. Of these the most important are range, sensitivity, and the type of water. Most still water floats have the main buoyancy at or near the bottom, or evenly spaced along the length of the float, as with the straight peacock type. For close range fishing in shallow still water, simple peacock quill or balsa floats with fine inserts made from thin cane, cocktail sticks, plastic bristles, or reversed crow or pheasant quill ends, are normally used (see Fig. 31).

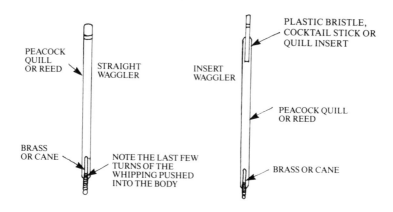

*Fig. 31. Constructing wagglers.*

These are light and sensitive and will show the slightest indication of a bite. A couple of dust shot or micro dust shot are all that will be used down the line, in favourable conditions. For fishing at longer range, in deeper water, or when windy conditions are encountered, stepped up and longer versions of the above floats are used, in some cases with the addition of a balsa body to increase the shot carrying capacity. Due to the range, inserts will need to be thicker for both visual and stability reasons, therefore reducing the sensitivity. On those rare occasions when the surface of the water is calm, it is possible to use bigger floats which will incorporate fine plastic, cane or reverse quill inserts, so a couple of these will be handy to have. (see Fig. 32).

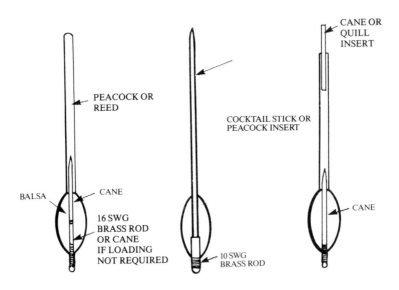

*Fig. 32. Bodied wagglers.*

For really difficult windy conditions, an antenna float with a sight bulb on a fine cane or fibreglass stem is a useful item. These are normally fished with the bulk of the shots down the line and a No. 4 or BB shot hard on the bottom. Bites are often signalled by the float lifting high out of the water when this bottom shot is moved by a taking fish (see Fig. 33). The same method can be used with similar floats which have a plain thin stem and balsa body without the sight bulb. These would be used in calmer conditions.

Looking at the floats that are fished top and bottom and the materials used in their construction, the most complex of these is the stick float. Unfortunately many of the stick floats sold in tackle shops are of no use for fishing in the manner for which they are designed, that is to present a bait at the speed the fish want, and to indicate a bite from the moment the tackle hits the water to when the float is fully cocked. To achieve this the float

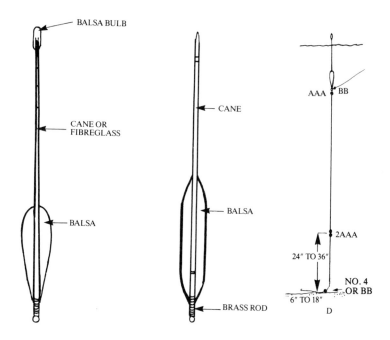

*Fig. 33. Antenna floats.*

must be made of cane and balsa of the correct diameter and density and in the correct proportions to each other. A correctly made and balanced stick float pivots from a point approximately 10 mm below the float tip and it is this pivoting action which makes the float work (see Fig. 34). At no time is there more than 5 mm of float above the surface. If a fish intercepts the bait as it is falling through the water, the bite is registered immediately by the float tip disappearing below the surface.

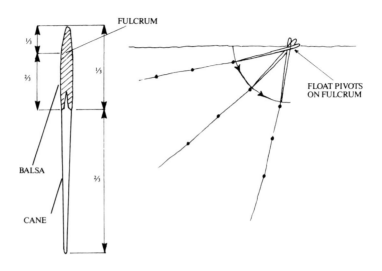

*Fig. 34. Principle of the stick float.*

When making the traditional cane and balsa stick floats, two-thirds cane and one-third balsa is the correct proportion of materials to use. The cane and balsa are spigotted, assembled, and glued before shaping. High density split cane must be used for making stick floats, and tapered to suit. This can be obtained from garden shops and is normally painted green. Cane from old broken split cane rods can also be used. The thin round cane used to make inserts and stems of antenna floats is not suitable for stick floats as it is neither thick enough nor heavy enough. When buying stick floats always ensure they have a heavy feel to the stem when held horizontally with the tip between the fingers. If they feel light, avoid them.

A good alternative to the cane and balsa stick float is the wire stem stick. Unlike the cane and balsa stick float, which always has a standard taper, wire stem sticks can also be made with a reversed taper (see Fig. 35). These are ideal for slow flowing waters where a more sensitive tip is an advantage. The wire stem float with the standard taper is excellent for fishing flowing water which is on the turbulent side, i.e. with boils and swirls as opposed to a smooth glide. The reduced cross-sectional area of the stem helps the float to ride through the swim without being pulled under by the turbulence and giving 'false' bites. Body lengths can vary from 50 mm in length in steps of 5 mm to 80 mm. Once this length is reached it is advisable to increase the diameter of the balsa from 6 mm to 8 or 10 mm if heavier floats are required.

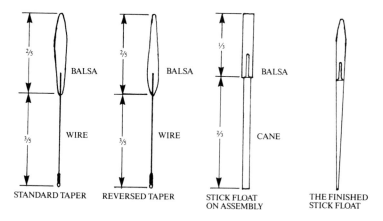

*Fig. 35. Construction of stick float.*

Avon floats are made by using either quill or cane stems with balsa or cork bodies (see Fig. 36). Note the position of the body in relation to the length of the quill or cane. The length of body should not exceed one-third of the total float length, otherwise the float will become unstable. It is always positioned about 25 – 30 mm from the top of the stem. If a thick top is required on an Avon float to make it more visible when fishing at long range, this can be achieved without using thicker quill or cane stems. A piece cut from the end of a goose or heron quill can be inserted into the top of the body (see Fig. 36) and glued into position.

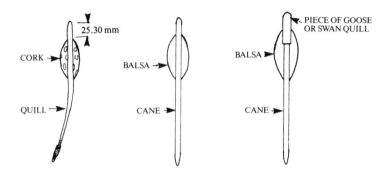

*Fig. 36. Construction of Avon floats.*

The most uncomplicated of the balsa floats to make is the simple trotting type. These can be made from 6 mm or 8 mm dowel for a slim close range float, or from 10 mm or 12 mm dowel for the dumpy chub type trotters used for supporting large baits in very fast flowing rivers (see Fig. 37). A stronger bottom can be achieved by drilling the balsa before shaping it and glueing in a short piece of cane. The balsa can then be tapered to give a smooth line.

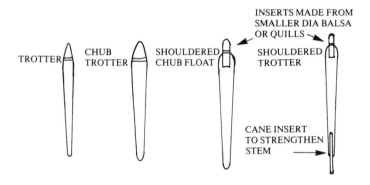

*Fig. 37. Construction of balsa trotters.*

Straight balsa floats have a habit of riding out of the water if held back. One way to overcome this tendency is to make a shoulder below the tip. The water will then act on this shoulder, holding the float down. The best way to do this is to drill and shape the balsa and then to cement in a piece of quill or smaller diameter dowel. This will make a stronger top than trying to form the shoulder and tip from solid balsa. It is also quicker and neater.

These then are just a few of the wide range of floats available. One advantage of making your own is that should you come up against a situation which cannot be overcome by using a commercial pattern, familiarity with the raw materials and an understanding of their various qualities will enable you to devise a 'special' of your own design to help you solve the problem. Sometimes, as I have done with my insert wire stem float, an existing commercial float can be modified rather than making a complete float from scratch.

## Assessing Your Swim

One important function that is essential to successful float fishing is to establish the geography of the swim in front of you. Continental anglers spend up to 15 minutes establishing this before they start to feed or fish, and their matches are normally of only two hours' duration as opposed to the 5 hours average duration of English matches, a much higher proportion of their match time. This can only emphasise the importance of this essential function. Obviously if the venue is well known to you, the various features of the swim will also be known and you will only have to spend time reminding yourself of their exact position and depth. But if the water is new to you it is essential to 'plumb' around to find any shelves, ledges, bars, gulleys, etc, not just in front of you but also at long range. I remember the first time I fished a certain gravel pit in a club match.

Fortunately I went to investigate the water a few days before the match. The bank dropped off steeply from the edge down to about 10′ in depth. This was maintained to about 4 or 5 rod lengths out. Due to the time of year and the type of fish the water held, I did not expect to find many fish in that depth of water. After a fruitless couple of hours trying close in on the pole and out on the 5 rod length mark, I set up a swing tip rod and cast well out. I was surprised when the tip fell back after a count of about 4. At my rate of counting, which is about a unit per foot, this meant a depth of 4′ at about 40 yards out. By casting progressively shorter for several more casts, I established that the pit shelved up to this depth from 10′ at about 30 yards or 7 rod lengths out, and by putting on a bigger waggler, I was able to reach this comfortably with my float and feed with a catapult. I fished at 7′ deep half-way up the ledge in about 6′ of water, and immediately started to catch fish. After about an hour, as sport slowed, I lengthened off back to 10′, and using my indicating shot as a plummet, I brought the tackle back a twitch at a time until it acted on my float tip (see Fig. 38). This meant I was just at the point where the bottom of the shelf began. I then started to pick up a better class of fish, including the odd bream. I have related these events in an attempt to explain alternative ways of 'plumbing' the depth without actually using a traditional plummet. At long range it is very difficult to cast the distance with a plummet, especially in deep water. But by understanding your shotting and the effect of it on the float, or the timing of the fall of a leger weight through the water, you can still establish the geography of the water quickly and effectively at both the beginning and during the course of a match as and when changes are necessary.

When using a waggler at long range in flowing water, the way to plumb the depth is quite straightforward. Set up the float and shotting so that the float is almost fully trimmed but will still

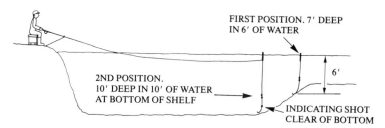

*Fig. 38. Assessing your swim.*

carry a No. 4 shot without going under. Nip a No. 4 shot just above the hook and cast in. Allow the float to go through the swim unhindered. If you are too shallow the float will travel through without going under. Move the float up a foot at a time until the shot drags bottom. When it does the float will pull under and you will then have the depth of your swim to within a few inches. You then remove the No. 4, trim the float to the required setting and start fishing, noting the position of the float with regard to the ring spacings on your rod when the hook is level with your reel. If you alter your depth or get broken off at any time during the match you can then quickly re-set your position without having to re-plumb. This rule also applies when fishing still water.

# 4 LEGERING

As previously mentioned, legering has seen a much greater revolution in the development of methods and equipment than any other branch of the sport. It is essential for any aspiring match angler to take it very seriously and to master every aspect of it. The old days when anglers looked upon it as a fall-back method only to be considered as a last resort, are long gone. For those anglers who are prepared to work hard at mastering the method of using leger tactics, the rewards can be considerable. I emphasise the word 'work'. The angler who casts in a leger rig and then sits back and waits for things to happen, is not only throwing away his chances, but is also failing to understand how potent a method legering can be in skilled hands. As in float fishing, you can sit back and wait or you can work and make things happen. It is not by chance that many of our top float anglers are also top leger men. The reason they are so successful is because they adopt the same philosophy and attitude to legering as they do to float fishing. In this chapter I intend to cover the methods and the tactics together, in the hope of giving a more complete picture of both the method and its potential.

## Still Water Legering

I am deliberately dealing with still water legering and flowing water legering separately, as the methods, tactics and major equipment such as rods, vary so widely. They are two different ball games, although the terminal tackle can be very similar. The most important thing to remember about terminal tackle is to keep it simple and to avoid any unnecessary use of ironmongery. Swivels have a very limited place in terminal tackle for match fishing. When used with fine soft lines, any possible advantage they may have in preventing the line from kinking is more than outweighed by the disadvantage of creating a focus point around which the line will tangle, and any weed or floating debris will collect, thus rendering them useless by preventing them from turning, as they are intended to do. The three rigs shown in Fig. 39 will cover most legering situations used in still water and flowing water, with only the length of tail and link needing to be modified.

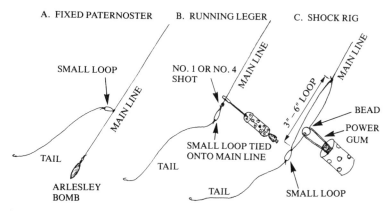

*Fig. 39. Leger and feeder rigs.*

For straight legering in still water and flowing water, the simple fixed paternoster is by far the most effective set-up. The two feeder rigs will be explained in detail later. Let us assume that we are using the fixed paternoster on still water, with a swing tip as our bite indicator. To make the loop in the line for a paternoster, use the knot shown in Fig. 40. The reel line is doubled over and then wrapped around itself about 3 – 4 times. The end is pushed through the loop so that about 12 mm (½ ") protrudes. Then by pulling from the other end you tighten the coils, trapping the line, so that a loop is left to which you tie your tail line. The length of line remaining is trimmed to the length you want your link to be, and your bomb is then tied to the end.

The length of the tail and link is governed by the way the fish are feeding or by the presentation of the bait that you require. When fishing for bream or roach in still water, especially in the warmer months, you can expect the fish to be feeding off as well as on the bottom. A slowly falling bait can be more attractive to these fish than a bait just lying on the bottom. In this case a tail as long as 6′ may be used to obtain this falling effect. This would be used in conjunction with a link of about 12″ long (see Fig. 39A). If whilst using this rig you find that the bait is being sucked or taken by the fish and you are not seeing any indication on the tip, then you must shorten the length of the tail to 3 − 4′ in the hope of the bite registering properly on the tip. When you

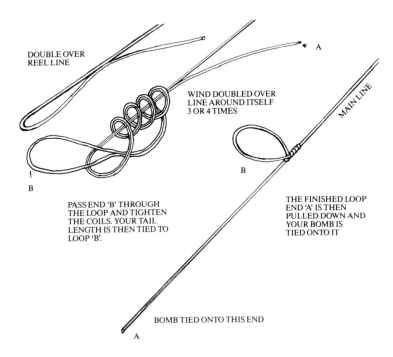

*Fig. 40. Tying a paternoster loop.*

are fishing on the drop in this way it is important that your line is tightened up to the bomb at all times, otherwise a bite will not register. When the bomb hits the bottom the reel line goes slack. This is the critical moment. You must take the slack out of the line but at the same time see any bites that may occur. Although the bomb has hit the river bed, the tail will still be slowly falling through the water, and it is at this time you are likely to get a bite.

The way to do it is this: you over cast the baited area by several yards. As soon as the bomb hits the surface of the water you engage the pick-up and put the rod onto the rod rests. As the bomb falls through the water it will be drawn towards you in an arc before hitting the baited area. Whilst it is falling it will pull your swing tip out straight (see Fig. 41A). As it hits the river bed the tip will collapse. It is at this point you must start taking in slack line, but at the same time you must be looking out for bites. This is achieved by gently and smoothly winding in the slack line, at the same time trying to keep the tip at the same angle (see Fig. 41B). With practise you will do this. If the tip rises you will know by the feel whether it is because all the slack has been taken up or because a fish has intercepted the bait. If the tip rises sharply whilst you are winding in gently, it must be a bite, so strike.

If a bite does not show on the drop and you know your bait is now lying on the bottom, you must lift the rod gently and move the bomb a few feet towards you. This is to straighten out the tail. It will probably have fallen in a heap with the line coiled or snaked. You must straighten this so that if a fish picks up the bait the tip will move immediately (see Fig. 41C). If after several minutes the bait has still not been taken, gently lift the bomb again, which in turn lifts the tail, causing the bait to rise in the water and then to slowly settle again. Continue to do this every few minutes until you know the bait has been pulled through the baited area. You can then wind in and recast. Very often it is as the bait is settling again after a lift that a fish sees it, takes it, and a bite is registered (Fig. 41D).

In the colder months when water temperatures are very low, the fish will not be moving around in the water as freely as they do when the water is warm. If you can get them bites will be very shy, so the length of the tail is kept down to 2 – 3′ in length. The link is reduced to about 9″ in still water and to 6″ in flowing water, and the bait is left much longer between lifts, as continual casting across the water will unsettle the fish and make them even more reluctant to feed.

When you set up your rod rests for swing tipping you will need up to three rests to support your rod properly. Avoid rod rests with fork tops and thin stems. The best rod rests are the wide type with polythene tubing stretched across the top, or better still the snag free round type shown in Fig. 45. These are bought separately from the bank sticks into which they screw. A good bank stick is made of aluminium tube of at least 12 mm diameter with a brass insert on the end into which the rod rest head is screwed. The all-in-one type of rod rests with the V tops and thin stems are useless. They spin round or collapse causing your rod to fall into the water, or your line snags around the ends causing it to snap when you strike. This loses tackle and fish, both of which are valuable. Never have more than 12″ of rod tip hanging over the end of the rod rest when legering, otherwise you will lose the sensitivity of the tip due to it bouncing about in the wind. Position the rod pointing downsteam if the water has any undertow or a slight flow, at an angle of 90° – 120° to the line (see Fig. 42). This is the most effective angle when striking to set the hook home. When you tighten your line to the bomb your swing tip should be set just off the vertical (see Fig. 41C). This is so that if a fish swims towards you with the bait the tip will fall back, indicating that the bomb has been moved. If this happens, strike.

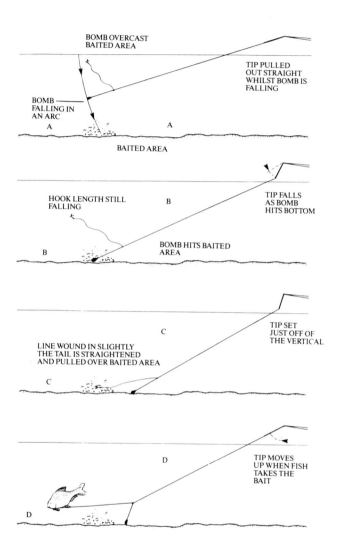

BOMB OVERCAST
BAITED AREA

TIP PULLED
OUT STRAIGHT
WHILST BOMB IS
FALLING

BOMB
FALLING IN
AN ARC

A

A

BAITED AREA

HOOK LENGTH STILL
FALLING

B

TIP FALLS
AS BOMB
HITS BOTTOM

BOMB HITS BAITED
AREA

B

C

TIP SET
JUST OFF OF
THE VERTICAL

LINE WOUND IN SLIGHTLY
THE TAIL IS STRAIGHTENED
AND PULLED OVER BAITED AREA

C

D

TIP MOVES
UP WHEN FISH
TAKES THE
BAIT

D

*Fig. 41. Swingtipping.*

The swing tip should also be positioned just above the surface of the water, if possible. Sometimes because of marginal weed growth you need to have it higher so that the line is clear of the weeds when it enters the water. If possible, provided the water is not deep or the shelf is not too steep, it pays to wade out and clear a channel through the weed so that your line can lie unhindered in the water. To do this, fit a weed cutting attachment to your landing net handle. Always take care whenever you start to wade for any reason. Test the river bed in front of you with the aid of your landing net handle. Make sure it does not drop away suddenly, and that the bottom is firm. If you have any doubts, do not wade.

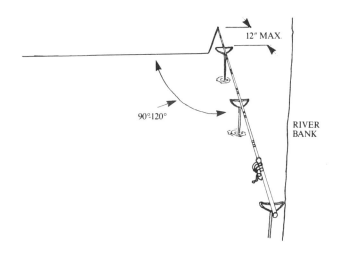

*Fig. 42. Correct positioning of rod when tipping.*

Some rivers, such as the Witham and the Nene and some of the Fen drains, are run off as the tide turns. This run off is controlled by large sluice gates being opened and closed. This means that the river can be still when you start to fish and then suddenly start moving slowly. Sometimes if a surplus of water is allowed into the river but the main sluice is closed, the river can even back up and go the 'wrong' way. These movements are indicated by the swing tip being drawn out and not settling back as normal. Wind and undertow can also cause this. In these circumstances you need to do one of two things; either fit on a longer tip or weight the tip with lead wire to act against the pull, or fit a moulded rubber link in place of the silicone rubber tube (see Fig. 43). You also need to do this in very windy weather to stop the tip being blown about, otherwise it becomes very difficult to pick out the movements which show a bite. Of the two methods I prefer to use the moulded rubber link. It is very effective, and many of the top match anglers have adopted its use in preference to the old method of weighting the tip with lead wire. These links can be bought separately from the tips in packets of 3 or 4, each link being of a different strength. Always use the weakest that conditions allow. The strongest of the set will cope with quite a good strength of flow before straightening out, but I would normally switch to another form of indication in preference to using a really strong swing tip link. This is because a very strong link can affect both the range and accuracy of the cast to a certain degree.

Sometimes when swing tipping in still water, either due to being on a high bank or because of the depth of the water, the angle of the line coming out of the water to the swing tip is too shallow to make bite indication possible (see Fig. 44). In these circumstances either a long parallel quiver tip or a spring tip can be used. In still or slow flowing water under these conditions the spring tip is by far the more sensitive. Due to the hinge action produced by the spring being at the bottom of the indicator, there is no progressive resistance for a taking fish to feel. Bites are positive and hittable. Several sizes of spring tip can be used, the size being classified by the length of the tip and the strength of the spring, the two factors which determine the sensitivity of the tip.

Although over the past few years the use of a swing tip has become less fashionable, in favour of the quiver tip, I still feel that for bream fishing or for fishing for other large fish such as

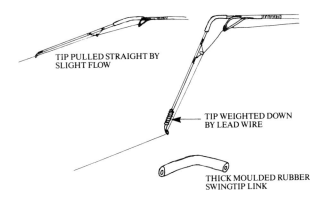

TIP PULLED STRAIGHT BY
SLIGHT FLOW

TIP WEIGHTED DOWN
BY LEAD WIRE

THICK MOULDED RUBBER
SWINGTIP LINK

*Fig. 43. Weighting the tip or using moulded link.*

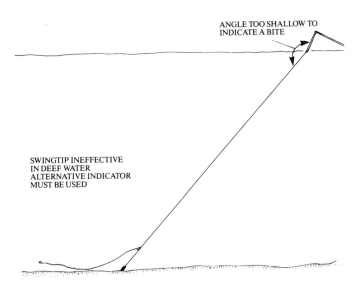

ANGLE TOO SHALLOW TO
INDICATE A BITE

SWINGTIP INEFFECTIVE
IN DEEP WATER
ALTERNATIVE INDICATOR
MUST BE USED

*Fig. 44. Ineffective angle of tip.*

tench or quality roach where confident bites are expected, it is
superior to any other form of indicator. The fish are less likely
to drop the bait due to feeling the resistance of the indicator, as
often happens with a quiver tip, and consequently the angler can

allow more time between seeing the indication and striking. This is particularly important when encountering the problem of line bites. These are caused by fish, especially bream, moving into or through the swim and catching the submerged line with their bodies. They are normally indicated by rapid lifts and fall-backs of the swing tip instead of by the normal preliminary knocks which are followed by a smooth and positive lift. With a quiver tip it is much more difficult to distinguish these differences, and the last thing you want to do if bream are moving into the swim is to strike at false bites and unsettle the fish. The only time a quiver tip should be used in normal still water situations is when bites are very shy or small fish are the likely quarry. In this situation use a soft parallel quiver tip for long range legering or a specially designed wand for close range.

Regarding the type of rods used for legering in still water. As described in the chapter on equipment, a classic tip to through action rod of about 9½' to 10' in length with a screw socket incorporated in the tip ring, is all that is needed for the straight legering or light feeder work usually appropriate when match fishing on still waters or slow moving drains and canals. This allows the use of a wide variety of indicators such as swing tips, spring tips and quiver tips.

If it is thought that a purpose built quiver tip rod is needed for those occasions when bites are extremely shy, one of the super sensitive wands which have a range of three or four tips of different strengths should be considered. These allow you to fish with the very light bombs and fine bottoms which are essential in those conditions. The range of tips will also cover close range legering in flowing water where a stronger tip is required than in still water. A top quality wand is shown in Fig. 3. Ideally only a slight curve is needed on the quiver tip to allow the bite to indicate. The rod tip must be properly supported to stop it bending with the tip and to stabilise it in windy conditions.

Excessive overhang of the rod tip will make bite indication very difficult to detect. One way of easily detecting very shy bites and protecting the tip from the worst effect of wind is to use a target board. These can be made from formica or thin perspex but should not be too gaudy. They are best painted matt black with lines of a dull colour which will give enough contrast without dazzling or giving eye strain (see Fig. 45).

*Fig. 45. Correctly supported 'Q' tip rod and target board.*

## Feeder Fishing in Still Water

Using a swim feeder on still water has several positive advantages. It allows a precisely metered rate of feed to be used, concentrated around the hook bait, regardless of the range at which you are fishing or the wind conditions, and on waters that do not respond to ground bait, you are still able to introduce feed beyond the range of your catapult, and in a tighter area. This is assuming, of course, that your casting is accurate. To aid in this it is essential to try to pick out a feature in the water to use as a marker. It could be a reflection in the water, a distant weed bed, or some feature on the far bank with which to line up your cast. These hints also apply to the positioning of your tackle and feed, regardless of the method being used. Two basic types of swim feeder are used. The block-end for introducing maggots, and the open end for using ground bait mixed with inert baits such as casters, hempseed and squatts. These come in a wide range of patterns and sizes, a few of which can be used as bought but many more which require modifications of one sort or another. These modifications apply particularly to the linkages. Except for the block-end type which use a central thick nylon link with interchangeable non-toxic weights (see Fig. 39B), most others which use plastic, wire, nylon line or some other form of link, need modifying if constant tangles or the use of swivels and split links are to be avoided. I use the same type of linkage on all my open-ended feeders from the smallest still water one to the giant 3 – 4 oz fast water type. It consists of a 3 – 4 mm diameter bead running freely on a 4" to 5" length of power gum which has been doubled over and tied to form an

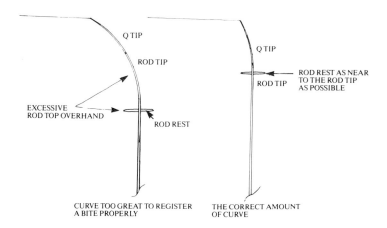

*Fig. 46. Correctly and incorrectly supported tip.*

endless loop. The knot is then slipped under the lead flap of the feeder in place of the original link and reclamped (see Fig. 47).

When fitted to the line, the line goes through the same hole in the bead as the power gum. I have tried the leger beads with a second raised eye moulded onto the bead, but have found them too prone to tangling. Even when sharing the same hole as the power gum, the bead slides easily up and down the main line. So why introduce additional complications?

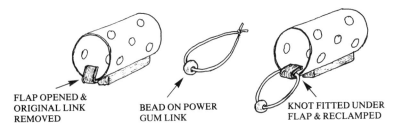

FLAP OPENED &
ORIGINAL LINK                BEAD ON POWER              KNOT FITTED UNDER
REMOVED                      GUM LINK                   FLAP & RECLAMPED

*Fig. 47. Fitting power gum links.*

In extreme conditions of low water temperature or when very little loose feed should be introduced, the very small conical feeders can be used in conjunction with an Arlesley bomb (see Fig. 48).

These have no built in-weight, so can be slid onto the link of the basic paternoster set-up. Between the loop and the bomb a No. 4 split shot should be fitted half an inch above the cap to stop the feeder sliding up to the loop and tangling on the cast. The half inch gap allows the top of the feeder to be opened for loading with bait samples. When using maggots in a block end feeder, always change the hook bait first before filling the feeder. Otherwise the feeder will empty before you have chance to cast. To reduce the rate that a block end feeder empties, wrap insulation tape around the body, reducing the number of holes.

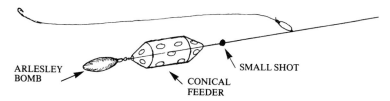

ARLESLEY BOMB          CONICAL FEEDER          SMALL SHOT

*Fig. 48. Conical feeder and Arlesley bomb.*

When using ground bait in an open-ended feeder, mix the ground bait with as little water as possible. This has the effect of making the ground bait explode out of the feeder, as opposed to gradually falling out on the bottom, and creates an attractive cloud of falling particles. In the first 15 – 20 minutes of a match, constant casting at one to two minute intervals is essential when the fish are expected to feed freely. This ensures that a good carpet of feed is laid on the bottom to hold the interest of the fish when they arrive in the swim. This is especially important when fishing for larger shoal fish such as bream or tench or when fishing evening matches, which are often of shorter duration. Once you have laid this bed of feed down, if you feel that the splash of a feeder or the continual introduction of ground bait could unsettle the fish, particularly in shallow water, you must remove the feeder and use a straight paternoster set-up. If you have the luxury of two still-water legering rods, then obviously it saves time to have one set up with a feeder and one with a straight paternoster rig, alternating from one to the other as the situation dictates.

## Legering on Flowing Water

If you intend to compete effectively on flowing water, you must be prepared to invest in a much larger range of equipment. Due to the wide variations in conditions to be found in rivers throughout the season, at least three, or probably four different types of rod will be needed. Because of the forces encountered when legering in flowing water, most of these will have to be carbon. The stiff properties of carbon rods make them far superior to fibreglass for this sort of work. The deciding factor in the choice of rod is the rate of flow and the range you intend to fish. This can vary considerably down the length of a river, especially if it has tidal reaches, and of course at any given place due to flood conditions.

Let me tell you how my collection of rods came about, as I feel this will best illustrate the points I am making.

For many years, due to my geographical location at the time, most of my fishing centred around still waters or slow moving rivers and drains. I only needed two leger rods – a classic through action bream rod with screwed tip ring to take a variety of indicators, and a tip action quiver tip rod with a spliced-in quiver tip capable of handling small leger weights in slow moving or moderate flows. My move to South Yorkshire coincided with the development of long range feeder tactics as a winning method on the river Trent, both in the middle reaches around Nottingham, and on the tidal stretches between Collingham and Gainsborough. My quiver tip rod was useless on this river for anything but fishing a small feeder down the side. It was not capable of casting a heavy feeder at any distance, and the tip was too soft to hold out in any appreciable rate of flow without bending too far over and rendering it ineffective. By investing in an 11′ carbon quiver tip rod, I was able to fish effectively with a medium size feeder up to 1½ oz in the middle reaches and up to half-way across, but on the tidal stretches or in winter conditions on the middle reaches it had insufficient power. Neither could I fish at very long range on the wider middle reaches in normal conditions. I overcame this problem by buying a 13′ fibreglass float rod blank, and by cutting and splicing the top and middle sections, produced a rod of about 11¼′ in length, with sufficient power to cast a 4 oz heavy feeder well across the river, and with enough sensitivity in the tip to indicate the bites. Note that no quiver tip was fitted or spliced in. All indication was direct to the rod tip. This rod has coped with most of the extremes of flow encountered, apart from the lower tidal reaches, where I found that at long range or when the river was carrying extra water, although I could cast a heavy enough feeder to where I wanted it, the tip was pulled round to its limit by the flow and was only capable of indicating drop back bites. Consequently I had to rig my terminal tackle in such a way that 90% of bites would be drop backs. This will be explained more fully later. The only way to overcome this problem was to buy yet another leger rod, this time a heavy carbon feeder rod. The action is similar to my home made fibreglass rod, but as the tip is carbon as opposed to fibreglass, the extra stiffness allowed the 10% of pull bites I was missing with the fibreglass rod, to be indicated.

For the benefit of anyone who would like to convert a redundant fibreglass float rod into a heavy feeder rod, the basic guidelines are shown in Fig. 49. A number of friends have followed this procedure and have produced a quite acceptable weapon. The very tip of the rod above the top splice needs to have a much closer ring spacing than before to make it indicate correctly.

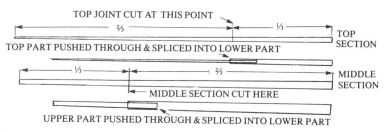

*Fig. 49. Converting a 13' float rod into a feeder rod.*

When Straight Legering, the terminal tackle used in flowing

water is basically the same as in still water. The paternoster is still the best set up in most conditions, with the only difference being the lengths of tail and link, and in certain conditions the type of leger weight. In flowing water the tail and link is much shorter, 12 – 18" being the normal starting length of tail, with a 6 – 9" link.

Normally when fishing at close to medium range, one or two SSG shot clipped to the link make a very effective and cheap form of leger weight. If, due to the speed of the current you cannot hold the bait where you want it, a coffin lead or a capta lead can be used. When fishing at long range a slightly flattened Arlesley bomb can be used if you need to hold out. Capta leads, although very effective at holding bottom, are, due to their shape, awkward to cast any distance without tangling problems. When a rolling bait is needed to search the river bed in an arc from the centre of the river to the edge, a drilled bullet is the type of leger weight to use. This is slid directly onto the main line and stopped with a split shot to whatever length of tail you require. No link is needed when fishing this method. A light fibreglass quiver tip rod or a carbon quiver tip for heavier flows will be ideal for use with these leger weights.

Except when fishing down the side in flowing water, when the rod will be pointing straight out in front of you, it is normal practice to fish with the rod pointing downstream when legering in flowing water. Often, due to the size of your weight or feeder and the range at which you are fishing, the pressure of the water on your line can cause the quiver tip to bend too much. In this situation the rod will need to be lifted to a near vertical position so that the least amount of line possible is actually in the water, thus reducing the pressure on the tip. Obviously in very windy conditions this is not always possible, and it is in these situations that having another, stronger rod can give you the advantage.

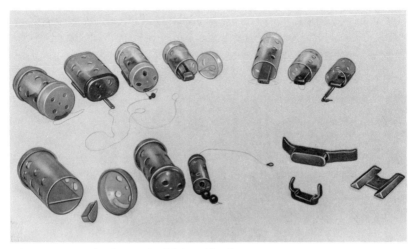

*Fig. 50. Swimfeeders and additional leads.*

**Feeder Fishing in Flowing Water**
Unlike when feeder fishing on still water, where casting distance normally determines the weight of the feeder, in flowing water this is controlled by the speed of the current and the pressure of the water on the line. Most feeder systems offer the facility of altering the weight of the feeder by changing the weight of the main strip, and final fine adjustments can be made by using small clip-on weights in addition to the main strip (see Fig. 50). In extreme conditions 'ski' leads can be added beneath the main strip to almost triple the weight of the feeder.

The best way to illustrate the method of trimming and fishing feeders properly, is to take you through a typical fishing situation.

Starting with the feeder set up as a basic running leger (see Fig. 39B), and loaded to the approximate capacity suited to the prevailing conditions, let us assume that the flow is running from right to left. The point immediately in front of you will be the 12 o'clock position (see Fig. 51).

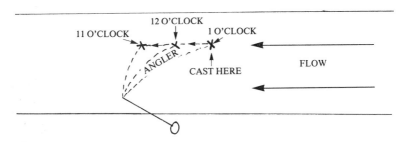

*Fig. 51. Positioning of rod for feeder fishing.*

Cast across and upstream to the 1 o'clock position. As soon as the feeder hits the surface, engage the pick-up and place the rod on the rest pointing downstream, and in fairly calm conditions up into the air. As the feeder falls through the water the tip of the rod will be bent over. When the feeder hits the bottom the line will go slack and the tip will straighten. As the current tightens the line the tip will start to bend again. As the pressure increases on the line the feeder will be moved, and this will be indicated by the tip straightening again. This rhythm should continue two or three times as the feeder bounces down the swim, until the feeder finally settles at a point between 12 o'clock and 11 o'clock, when hopefully the feeder will hold and the tip will curve over and stay in position. If the feeder continues to move, causing the tip to continue bouncing, more weight must be added to the feeder until it holds bottom where it should be. If on the other hand the feeder holds immediately between the 1 o'clock and 12 o'clock position, then the weight is too heavy and must be lightened. Having trimmed the feeder so that it settles in the correct area after two or three bounces, you can then start fishing.

As when fishing in still water, you must cast at regular one or two minute intervals in this opening period to lay an attractive carpet of bait on the bottom and consolidate the swim. Once this has been achieved the tackle can be left longer between casts, unless of course bites are forthcoming.

Bites can be indicated in a number of ways. The obvious ones are when the tip is pulled over sharply, well beyond the normal settling position, or by a series of jerks or taps. The less obvious ones are when the feeder fails to settle or hit the bottom, which means a fish has taken the bait on the drop, delaying or interrupting the natural fall of the feeder, or by a different rhythm of the rod tip as the feeder bounces through the swim to its normal resting position. Often a fourth bounce, when normally only two or three are registered, also means a bite. The bites I prefer are the drop backs. This is a sign that the fish are really feeding confidently, and that the feeder is properly trimmed. These are signalled by the tip falling back and straightening after the feeder has properly settled. This is due to the fish moving the feeder as it takes the bait, and these bites are generally guaranteed to produce a fish. A smooth firm lifting of the rod is all that is necessary to ensure the fish is properly hooked.

When I think the fish will be taking as confidently as this I use the terminal rig (shown in Fig. 39C). This is known as a shock rig. Instead of the feeder being allowed to run freely along the line, a long loop from 3″ to 6″ is tied in the line, after first threading on the feeder. This limits the travel of the line through the bead. When a fish takes the bait it acts like a bolt rig. This means that in most cases the fish virtually hooks itself against the weight of the feeder, which invariably moves it, and most indications are of the drop back type.

On many occasions when the fish will take the bait on the

move, bonus fish can be caught when sport slows, by deliberately moving the feeder to induce bites, as when we lift the tackle when legering in still water.

If after the feeder has settled no bites are forthcoming, by taking hold of the line just below the butt ring and pulling it gently but firmly, provided the feeder is properly trimmed it will start to move again. This can also be achieved by increasing the bow in the line, giving a greater amount of line for the water to pull against. As the feeder is moved the tip will fall back and then tighten again. Bites are signalled in the usual way, as either sharp taps, or by interruption in the normal rhythm of the rod tip. Obviously a great deal of practise is necessary before these methods are completely mastered, but as you can see, you only get out what you put in. When using really heavy feeders, normal three or four pound line should be used with a five or six pound B.S. shock leader to prevent cracking off on the cast. This means using about 5 metres of heavier line tied to the end of your reel line.

The really large open-ended feeders now in use on the Trent and Severn are easily made from plastic beer or soft drinks bottles. These are cut into 60 mm wide strips. If they are then cut into lengths of about 5″ (120 mm) they will make a swim feeder of about 40 mm diameter when overlapped and stapled (see Fig. 52A). Separate strip leads of various weights from 1 oz to 3 oz in half-ounce steps are now available in most good tackle shops, and a large feeder can thus be made for only the cost of the leads. The holes can be burned in with a small electric soldering iron, and two holes either side of the strip lead can be made with their centres the correct distance to take the small ¼ oz or ½ oz trim leads which are also now available (see Fig. 52C).

When using these really large feeders, the power gum and bead linkage already described is just as effective and tangles

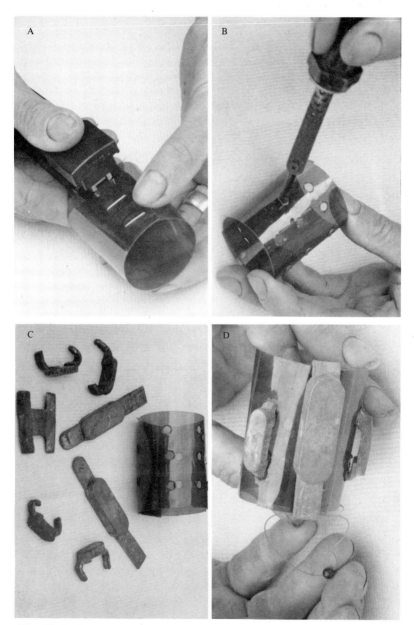

*Fig. 52. Making and weighting swimfeeders.*

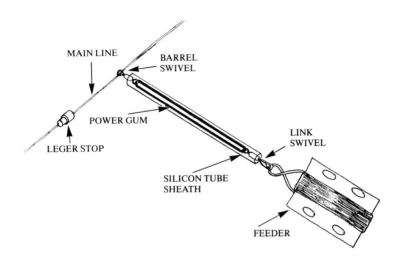

*Fig. 53. Feeder link incorporating swivels.*

are few and far between. If you would still feel happier using swivels and do not mind the additional expense and inconvenience, a rig incorporating a plain barrel swivel and a link swivel, connected by a power gum link is shown in Fig. 53. Note the silicon sheath that must be used to cover the swivels and help to prevent tangles.

# 5　POLE FISHING

When fishing on still water or flowing water where the fish can be brought within range, modern poles in the hands of accomplished anglers make rods and reels redundant in most match fishing situations within a radius of 10 – 11 metres of the peg. When I made this as then controversial statement at a National Squad meeting in 1976 (although the range quoted was only 8 metres at that time), I was almost lynched. But within one or two seasons, even my most severe critics became converts, and like many converts, too slavish to their new found beliefs than was good for them, often using this method to the exclusion of others more suitable for the prevailing conditions. But provided the techniques are learned, understood, and applied effectively when conditions are favourable, pole fishing is an essential and potent weapon in the match angler's armoury.

I have already covered in detail the qualities to be looked for when buying a pole, in the chapter on equipment. The object of this chapter is to cover the methods. As in previous chapters on float fishing and legering, I shall split the chapter into still water and flowing water applications once the general information has been dealt with.

When interest in pole fishing was rekindled in the early 'seventies, the main centre of use was in the southern part of the country, where traditional pole fishing to some minor degree had still been maintained in the Thames valley. The difference was that this renaissance was centred around continental methods rather than the traditional English style. What many anglers overlooked, despite their initial success, was that the continental style was developed around the use of bloodworm and jokers as bait, as opposed to fishing with maggots, casters, and punched bread. As the decade progressed and more and more anglers became proficient in using the methods, top class anglers such as Kevin Ashurst, who have international as well as national experience of the methods, began to realise the limitations of the continental approach and began to develop new methods more suited to our own waters and baits. This gave them an edge over those anglers who slavishly followed the continental methods on waters where bloodworm was either less effective as a match winning method or banned under local rules. I would recommend any angler who intends to take pole fishing seriously, to obtain a copy of Kevin Ashurst's excellent book *The Encyclopaedia of Pole Fishing* (Pelham Books), as obviously I cannot hope to cover in this brief chapter the invaluable information provided in a complete book.

Due to the intense physical and mental effort required to fish a pole effectively, the most important considerations when setting out equipment are efficiency and comfort. As previously mentioned, top pole anglers who specialise in fishing venues where the use of the pole is almost exclusive, often carry specially designed platforms on which to secure their seat box and equipment. As I fish many contrasting venues, I compromise with two adjustable legs bolted to the front of my box, as most situations present the problem of the bank sloping towards the waters edge.

Specialist items which are essential for pole fishing are pole rollers, rear hook rests, or when the bank allows, the excellent quick release pole holders which stick in the ground (see Fig. 54). Bait and tackle trays which fit on the sides and front of the seat box are also helpful, as is a good quality bait apron. An efficient lay-out for pole fishing is shown in Fig. 55. Note the position of the rear roller. Many anglers use a roller only in front of them, when in fact the roller was developed to keep the pole clear of the ground as it was being pushed backwards to land a fish.

Special short bank sticks are useful when the bank slopes upwards behind you.

*Fig. 54. Quick release pole holder.*

## Pole Tips

It is important never to shorten the top section of your pole to fit a crook or a PTFE bush. If you do, you will be unable to use the flick tip which is supplied with the pole. It is preferable to modify the crook or find the correct size of bush. Failing this the outside wall of the pole can be built up with whipping silk or Araldite until the diameter is suited to the bush, and the internal diameter will still receive the solid carbon flick tip. For those of you who have already committed this cardinal sin to your £500 carbon pole, deliverance is at hand. Shakespeare and several other companies have introduced some very fine carbon whips which incorporate a number of short, slow taper telescopic sections. You should have no difficulty in finding a combination of these which will slide into the remaining upper sections of the pole without upsetting the balance, leaving you free to preserve your internal elastic system without having to dismantle it if conditions dictate the use of a flick tip in preference to your elastic shock absorber, which I will now explain.

*Fig. 55. Efficient equipment layout for pole fishing*

When the continental system first became popular in the 'seventies, the normal practice was to use an aluminium or fibreglass crook to which would be fitted your elastic shock absorber (see Fig. 57). To eliminate occasional tangling problems, a system of running the elastic inside the pole itself was developed. This had the added advantage of allowing the use of an almost unlimited length of elastic, depending on how many sections you allowed the elastic to run through, which in turn depended on the size of fish you expected to encounter.

Many anglers saw the advantage of this and modified their poles accordingly, in many cases shortening the upper hollow section

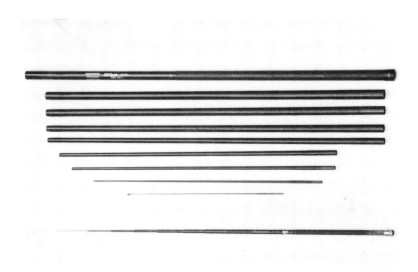

*Fig. 56. Carbon poles and whip.*

to suit the bushes which became available. This was fine if larger fish were the main quarry, but they soon encountered problems when speed fishing at longer range for small fish. Up to 5 or 6 metres, the range of telescopic poles available could be used, but for catching small fish with 8 – 11 metre take-apart poles which had been converted to internal elastic systems, they experienced a large proportion of fish being 'bumped off', as the elastic prevented efficient hooking due to the low resistance of the smaller fish against the strike. Even if they were able to fit flick tips into the end of the hollow section, it meant dismantling the complex internal shock absorber system which they may need to use later in the match. This is of course assuming that they could not afford a matched pair of poles, or at least a spare set of top sections, which are obviously not cost effective for the average club angler. Figure 58 shows a modern internal shock absorber system.

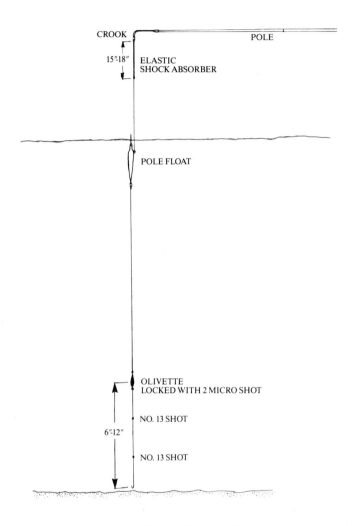

*Fig. 57. Bottom fishing continental style. The crook has now been superseded by the use of the internal elastic system.*

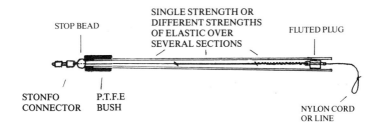

*Fig. 58. Pole top conversion kit.*

The elastic is run through the centre of the pole. For most situations the length of the first hollow section is normally sufficient, but in situations where larger fish can be expected, the elastic can be run through the top two or even three sections if necessary. On the end of the first hollow section a PTFE bush is fitted. This is superior to the earlier plastic, and slows down the rate at which it is drawn out of the bush by a fighting fish without causing any damage or fraying to the elastic. The amount of resistance can be governed to a large extent by altering the angle of the line to the pole tip (see Fig. 59).

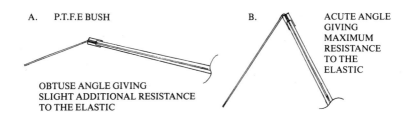

*Fig. 59. Altering angle of pole tip to vary resistance.*

If a large fish is hooked, by pointing the pole towards the fish as it runs, the possibility of breakage is reduced by allowing the elastic to stretch without too much added resistance, then by gradually altering the angle of the pole as the fish slows down, the pressure caused by natural resistance of the elastic can be increased gradually by increasing the resistance of the elastic moving over the lip of the bush. It is very difficult to explain this in text, and the best way to understand these points is by experimentation. After rigging up your system, hold the pole top in the right hand and pull the elastic out at the angle shown in Fig. 59A, noting the resistance of the elastic. Then release the elastic and repeat the exercise, this time pulling the elastic at the angle shown in Fig. 59B. The increase in resistance will be easily felt. If you look at the point where the elastic is being pulled out of the bush, you will see that the diameter of the elastic is drastically reduced as it is pulled over the lip of the bush (see Fig. 60). The strength of elastic required is dependent upon the breaking strain of your hook length (see chart). In very long systems where two or more sections are used, a progressive set-up using different strengths of elastic can be incorporated (see Fig. 58). Note that the finer elastic goes to the top of the pole. The normal strengths of elastic available are fine, medium, and

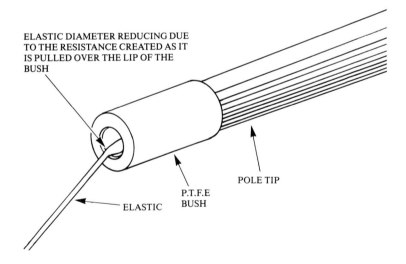

ELASTIC DIAMETER REDUCING DUE
TO THE RESISTANCE CREATED AS IT
IS PULLED OVER THE LIP OF THE
BUSH

POLE TIP

P.T.F.E
BUSH

ELASTIC

*Fig. 60. Elastic diameter reducing over bush lip.*

TWISTING ELASTIC IN OPPOSITE DIRECTIONS

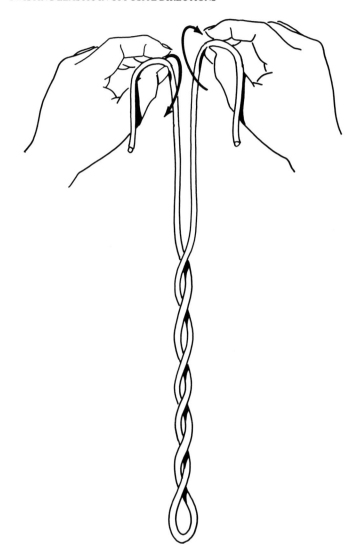

*Fig. 61. Doubling elastic.*

strong. In between or stronger strengths can be made by twisting the elastic between your fingers in opposite directions to double the strength (see Fig. 61). The loose ends are then tied together.

When the elastic is tied to the lower plug, which has a length of stiff nylon line or fly line backing attached for easy withdrawal from the pole, it is pulled out of the PTFE bush under slight tension and a small bead is slid over the elastic, running free between the bush and the plastic 'Stonfo' fitting which is then tied to it, and which is the standard quick release fitting (see Figs. 58 and 62). The plastic sleeve is then slid over the elastic, locking it in position. On the other end of the Stonfo connector is a hook in to which the tackle is looped, again being locked into position with a sliding sleeve. This allows a very quick change of tackle to be carried out when necessary.

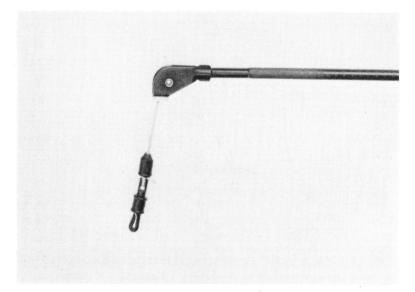

*Fig. 62. Quick release 'Stonfo' fitting. Note the new type roller fitting on the end of the pole, which incorporates a P.T.F.E. Bush. These are very efficient and highly recommended.*

## Pole Floats for Still Water Fishing

As when float fishing with rod and reel, a vast range of float patterns are now available, all claiming superiority in certain conditions. As in the float fishing chapter, I will restrict the selection to a few basic types, in the interests of both economy and brevity. At 60p to £1.50 each, anglers will obviously be more concerned with floats which catch fish rather than anglers. Once you have mastered the methods of using these few basic types, you will then be in a position to use your own judgement on the merits of other patterns.

The patterns under discussion can be divided into two areas; the type which use the continental system of olivettes, and those which have been developed for use with more traditional equipment and baits.

Looking at the continental systems first, which have been designed for use in deeper water and for taking fish on the bottom, the choice of float to be used is decided as when fishing with a rod and reel. It is largely dependent upon the type of water and the prevailing weather conditions. The length of pole to be used also has to be considered when choosing the size of the float. The longer the length of pole used, the larger the size of the float. This is to allow sufficient weight to cast out easily to the required distance.

If a light float is used with a long pole, especially in windy conditions, it will make control difficult and only result in tangles. Study the chart of suggested float sizes to pole lengths. Keep to this and no problems should arise. The pole floats can be limited to three basic types for bottom fishing, and a set of 4 or 5 different sizes of each type will be necessary (see Fig. 63).

Float A is the best pattern to use in deep still waters in fairly calm conditions. Float B can be used on still waters in most conditions and is the best type to buy if only one set can be

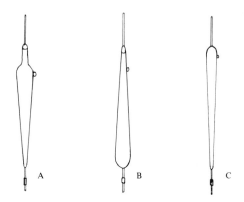

*Fig. 63. Pole floats.*

afforded initially. Float C is used in slow moving waters such as drains and canals, as well as in fast water. All three have certain things in common. They are all made of balsa wood, they all have fine bristle tips, and most importantly they all have fine wire eyes at the side of the floats near the top. All these floats are connected to the line at the top and bottom, enabling you to control the tackle properly from the pole tip. The float is held in position by a plastic float cap which slides over the bottom stem of the float. The length of fine bristle tip left showing is sensitive to only one No. 13 dust shot, so ultra sensitive shotting is required to set the float in the water so that only part of the bristle is showing. If silicon or rubber tube were used to connect the line at the top of the float, this would upset this fine balance at the tip due to the surface tension acting on the increased surface area of the rubber. The amount of extra shot needed to pull the rubber clear of the surface tension would exceed the shotting capacity of the float, and once the surface tension acting around the rubber was broken, the float would sink, rendering it useless.

To overcome this problem a very fine wire ring made from 5 amp fuse wire is fitted near the top of the float and the line is

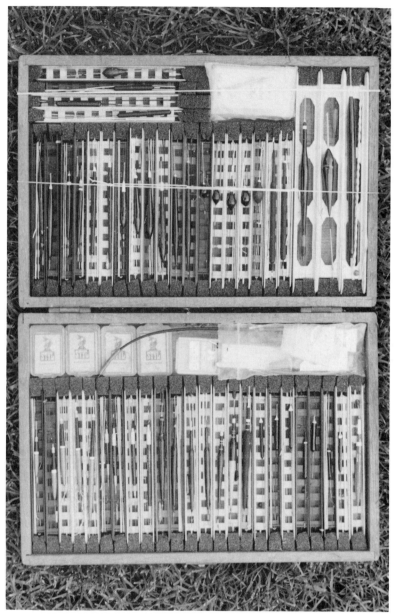

*Fig. 64. Pole tackles.*

threaded through this. This modification is sometimes needed to shop bought pole floats, although most of the imported continental floats are already fitted with this ring (see Fig. 68).

## The Olivette

This is the pear shaped weight used to form the bulk of the shotting capacity of the float. By concentrating the weight into this fine streamlined shape, casting out the tackle is made an easy tangle free operation, and the bait is quickly taken down to the fish. The olivettes are mounted on fine wires and when removed a tiny hole is left through the centre. It is then threaded on to the line and locked into position by placing a No. 10 or No. 12 micro dust shot on each side. The thinnest end should be pointed upwards towards the float.

Olivettes come in different sizes and are numbered 1, 2, 3, 4, 5, 6, etc, the lower numbers being the smaller weights. When setting up your tackle the floats must be matched accurately to the olivettes. Apart from the olivette and its two small locking shots, only two No. 13 micro dust shots are placed below it on the hook length (see Fig. 57). Let us say for example that we want to use a float which will take a No. 4 or 5 olivette. Looking at the chart on weight sizes to pole lengths, you can see that you will use this size when fishing with an 8 – 10 metre pole.

Using a deep water jug or tank for testing, you attach the No. 4 olivette to the bottom of the float with a short piece of line. The olivette should then be locked to the line with the same size of small shots you intend to use on the finished tackle. You now place the float and lead into the tank or jug. If the float sits in the water with more length of tip showing above the surface than the two No. 13 shots fixed on the hook length will pull down (see Fig. 65A), the bulk shot is too light, and you must now fit the next size of olivette, which in this case will be a No. 5. The chances are that this will be too heavy for the float and the float will sink to the bottom of the jug or tank (see Fig. 65B). This is fine. What you now have to do is to take a modelling knife and trim off pieces of metal from the olivette until the float rises to the surface and just a small amount (1 mm) of balsa tip is showing (see Fig. 65C). The float is now properly trimmed. When the tackle is made up and the two No. 13 shots are fitted to the hook length, the float will be set to its proper position. If it should sink or ride a little too low in the water, an additional light scraping of the olivette will do the trick. If it rides too high, replace the locking shots around the olivette with one or two shots of a slightly larger size.

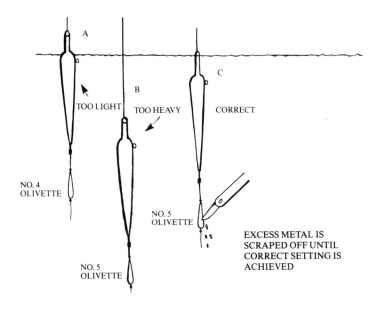

*Fig. 65. Trimming olivettes.*

Let us now look at the completed tackle set up. You have the stiff take-apart pole into which the elastic is fitted. To this the tackle is fitted by a loop being placed into the slot of the Stonfo fitting and held in place with the plastic sleeve. The elastic is

*Fig. 66. Holding a pole correctly.*

either fine, medium or heavy in strength. The strength of the elastic needed is determined by the size of fish you are expecting to catch and the size of hook and line being used. This balance is very important if you intend to fish effectively. As previously mentioned, the elastic acts as a shock absorber when playing the fish. It will stretch to almost six times its original length, cushioning the initial run of the fish and drawing it upwards through the water with a pumping action. Fish can be played out much quicker on a roach pole using elastic than with a rod and reel.

| Pole Length | | Float and Olivette Size | |
|---|---|---|---|
| 3 – 4 metres | | Size 0 – 2 | |
| 4 – 8 metres | | Size 2 – 4 | |
| 8 – 10 metres | | Size 4 – 6 | |
| 10 metres + | | Size 6 upwards | |
| Hook Size | Elastic | Main Line | Hook Length |
| 24 – 22 | Fine | 1 lb B.S. | 8 oz – 12 oz B.S. |
| 20 – 18 | Medium | 1 – 1½ lb B.S. | 12 oz – 1 lb B.S. |
| 18 – 16 | Medium to Strong | 1½ – 2 lb B.S. | 1 lb – 1½ lb B.S. |
| 16 – 14 | Extra Strong | 2 – 3 lb B.S. | 1½ lb – 2½ lb B.S. |

The floats as previously explained are selected to suit the type of water, and the size of float is dependent upon the length of pole to be used, along with the recommended size of olivette for that length of pole. The length of line between the pole top and the float should be kept as short as possible. The ideal way to use the pole is to control the tackle from directly above it. Bites are then connected with a smooth lifting of the pole tip as opposed to the conventional strike.

The length of pole needed is decided by the distance from the bank that you intend to fish and the depth of the water. The closer the fish can be brought into the bank the shorter the pole required. If fishing alongside the marginal weed of a river or pond a 4 – 5 metre pole will probably be sufficient. If you need to fish over the shelf on rivers such as the Witham or Welland, you may need an 8 – 10 metre length.

A large number of permutations of tackle length and size of olivette can soon be built up, but if you work on the principle that the further out you fish the deeper the water is likely to be, these can be cut down in number by having the smaller sizes of floats on shorter lines and the heavier tackle on longer lines.

The olivettes should be locked to the line just above the hook length. The hook length is seldom more than 6 – 12 inches in length. Two No. 13 microdust shot are spaced evenly along the hook length. If the bites are shy the shots can be moved together closer to the hook to give a more positive indication of a bite.

Several minutes of careful plumbing around the swim is essential for good results. Any holes or shelves should be located and noted and the tackle should be fished over these areas where possible. The float must be set so that the hook is exactly 15 – 25 mm off the bottom, so that when the fish move into the baited area, the bait on the hook will hit them smack between the eyes and the tackle will register immediately the bait has been taken.

When a fish is hooked and played on a pole, it may be necessary to remove sections to bring the fish in, especially when fishing a long pole in shallow water. This operation must be done smoothly (Fig. 67). The best way to do it is to slide the pole down across the thigh, removing the sections as you go, or to place the pole over the rear roller and feed it behind you, breaking the pole at the joint that will allow you to swing the fish into your hand. If a small fish has been hooked it will only be necessary to remove enough sections to allow the fish to be swung into your hand. If the fish is larger and requires netting, an additional section must be removed to allow the fish to be

*Fig. 67. Removing sections from a pole.*

drawn over the net without lifting it from the water.

If you are fishing from a steep or sloping bank, you may be unable to break down the pole by sliding the sections off and behind you. In these circumstances the pole must be brought around parallel to the bank and across the thigh, and the sections slid off from the side.

Never lift a hooked fish straight up and out of the water. Always bring it sideways away from the baited area before bringing it to the surface, otherwise the disturbance caused by the fish being brought across the surface will frighten the shoal.

When fishing with a long pole, the pole is held across the thigh, holding the pole down with the right hand behind the body and supporting it with the left hand under the pole in front of the knee (see Fig. 66). Never try to hold a long pole under your forearm as you would a rod. It will be totally unmanageable and difficult to hit your bites. This then is the basic method of bottom fishing continental style. Let us now look at the method for fishing around the surface, and mid-water areas.

The type of pole used for this style of fishing is known as a flick tip pole. The top joint is soft and has a tapered piece of solid fibreglass or carbon fibre fitted into the end, instead of being rigid as when bottom fishing. The pole can be a take-apart with a flick tip type top joint fitted, or can be of the telescopic type, or one of the new carbon whips. When buying a pole, a take-apart should be your priority. This type of pole can be used for bottom fishing or mid-water and surface fishing. As most of your pole fishing will be bottom fishing, this is the type for you. The telescopic type, although cheaper than the take-apart poles, can only be used for small fish using the flick tip method. They are too soft and floppy to use with elastic.

When using a flick tip pole, the line is connected to the end of the pole by a short length of line a couple of pounds heavier in breaking strain to the main line. This is because most of the shock and pressure is taken by the line closest to the tip, especially where it is connected to the small eye or string normally whipped to the end of the tip (see Fig. 56). No elastic shock absorber is used with this method, as it is mainly used for catching small fish such as bleak, small roach and gudgeon. The floats are also different. They are a lot finer and take very little shot, a sharp contrast to the heavier type used when bottom fishing.

The type I use are all home made, using small pieces of peacock quill with 24 or 22 gauge piano wire stems. For the really fine ones, the spring wire on which the olivettes are mounted can be used (see Fig. 68). A piece of fine 5 amp fuse wire is wrapped around a needle and the ends twisted together to make the eye. This is then glued to the side of the peacock to make the type of fine ring described earlier (see Fig. 68). The tops of the floats can be left flat or can have a short nylon or wire bristle. This must not be long, as used with the bottom floats, or the balance of the floats will be upset.

The small plastic float caps used to connect the float to the line can be made by cutting the plastic insulation from the very fine signal wires found inside connecting cables on hi-fi equipment and telephone cables. For fishing with long poles, balsa bodied floats made slightly larger and with heavier wire stems can be used. These are easier to cast than the light peacock type, but are not as sensitive.

When casting your pole tackle always use a side or underhand cast, casting into the wind, otherwise tangles will occur.

The shotting patterns used vary, depending on where in the water the fish are feeding. A loaded float can be used taking two No. 13 dust shots if fish are to be caught near the surface. A faster progressive fall can be achieved by using what is known as a logarithmic shotting pattern. This is used when fishing at mid-water in deep water, or when fishing near the bottom in shallow water. A range of shotting patterns is shown in Fig. 69. The length of line between float and pole tip can be short as described in the section on bottom fishing, or if speed fishing for bleak or small rudd and roach where the bite rate is very fast, the line can be left long enough to allow the fish to be swung into your hand without taking down sections of the pole. When using a telescopic pole the tackle has to be fished this way due to the difficulty in collapsing the pole. This again amplifies the limitations of the telescopic type of pole as against the versatility of the take-apart pole. Having said that, there are some excellent 4 and 5 metre carbon whips now available which are ideal for fishing in this way at close range.

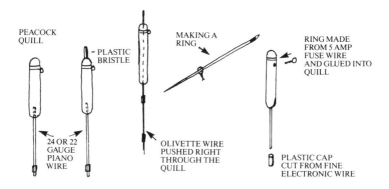

*Fig. 68. Floats for surface fishing, making an eye.*

Some poles have a line winding attachment whipped to the second or third section of the pole below the tip. This can be used whilst using a flick tip for shortening your length of line whilst fishing, and storing the surplus line until you need to lengthen it again. This is very useful if you have a limited number of readily assembled tackles, or if you intend to change your depth or range a number of times during the session.

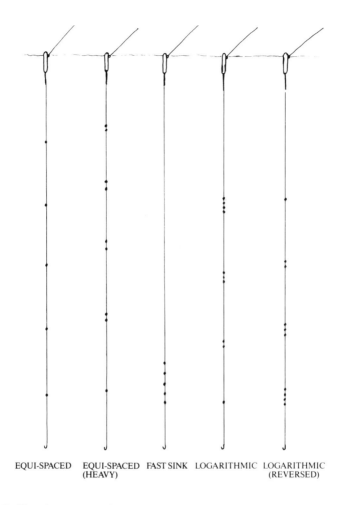

EQUI-SPACED    EQUI-SPACED   FAST SINK   LOGARITHMIC   LOGARITHMIC
               (HEAVY)                                 (REVERSED)

*Fig. 69. Shotting patterns for pole floats. Micro dust shot or style leads from size 10 to 13 are used.*

All the floats previously mentioned are connected to the line by the top and bottom, but sometimes due to surface drift or choppy conditions, a float which is connected to the line by the bottom end only is preferable. Terminal tackle is fished by laying on the bottom instead of just off the bottom as has been normal with previous rigs. The peacock quill and wire stem floats, with or without the short bristles, are ideal for this method.

The shotting patterns can vary as shown in Fig. 70. In conditions of average drift a small string of micro dust shots can be fished hard on the bottom. In less extreme conditions they can be fished clear of the bottom with the hook length lying hard on the bottom.

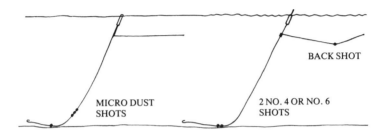

*Fig. 70. Laying on with the pole in still water.*

In really windy conditions a larger float which allows the use of much heavier shotting may be needed, using two No. 6 or No. 4 shots in place of the small string of micro-dust shot. If the water is really choppy, a mini-antenna type float made from slim balsa with a cocktail stick or plastic antenna can be used (see Fig. 71).

When using these methods, the line between pole tip and float needs to be $3' - 4'$ in length, depending on conditions. This is to prevent the tackle being jerked by the pole tip swaying in the wind. By leaving the line slack, the uncontrollable movements of the pole tip will not be transmitted to the tackle. A small back shot as shown in Fig. 70 will help to sink the line under the surface away from the worst effects of the wind. In very clear shallow water this extra length of line also means that the pole tip is not immediately above the tackle, and there is less chance of the fish being spooked by it.

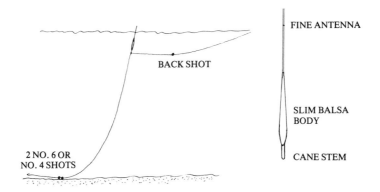

*Fig. 71. Using an antenna float.*

Practise and experience will show when these rigs perform better than the more traditional set-ups. Although I have described the rigs shown as still water rigs, most of them can be used or adapted for use in canals and slow moving drains. As you develop your skills and experience, don't be afraid to try new ideas and developments to overcome any localised situations. The rigs shown so far are not necessarily at the peak of their development and are still open to improvement and adaptation.

Because of the fineness of the tackle, most anglers make up their tackles at home and wind them on plastic winders, using different coloured winders as a code to the different lengths of tackle. To ensure that the winders unwind easily, it is important to wind the tackle on carefully. A centre peg is moulded into each end of the winder and the tackle below the float should be kept to one side of this. When the float has been wound on, cross over and wind the remaining line on to the other side.

When winding on a tackle which does not use elastic, the end can be held by slipping a piece of float rubber on the end of the line and sliding this over the peg. Winders can be bought in varying lengths, increasing in 1 cm stages. I normally keep to one size of winder at 14 cm. This holds most of the float sizes I use and can be stored more easily in slotted foam than a number of different sizes.

We have discussed using bleak whips for catching small fish, using a float to indicate the bite, but when actually fishing for bleak a float is only used as a casting weight. No matter how small and sensitive the float and no matter how quick the reactions of the angler, only a very small percentage of bites will be connected with by using the traditional method of indication and striking.

Due to the speed in which a bleak will suck in and blow out a bait at the slightest feel of resistance, a different approach must be adopted, and once perfected, tremendous weights of these small fish are possible. Providing the fish can be kept feeding throughout the match period, 10 to 20 lbs can be put on the scales.

As previously stated, the float is only used as a casting weight, and under normal conditions no shot is put down the line. The line is normally $1\frac{1}{2} - 2$ lb B.S. straight through to the hook which will be as large as you can get away with. Some people use barbless hooks but I prefer to squeeze down the barb of a standard fine wire crystal bend hook. This allows you to shake off the fish and the lump caused by squeezing down the barb helps to keep the maggot on.

A good floating line is essential and should be as new as possible. It must be almost as long as the whip or pole, allowing the fish to be swung in to your hand. The last 2′ is pulled across the thumb nail under tension. This causes the line to coil. The coils are then greased to make the line float better, and the increased diameter produced by the layer of grease helps to increase its visibility. Bite indication is by watching the coils straighten out as a fish takes the bait and a smooth lifting of the tip is all that is needed to connect with it.

When the water is clear, some anglers prefer to wear polarised sun glasses and watch the maggot slowly sinking, as soon as it disappears they strike. Old white maggots make the best hook bait, as they are tougher and last longer between changes. When a really high catch rate of 6 or more fish a minute is being attained, excessive bait changes can cost you several pounds of fish over the course of a 5 hour match. One big problem that often occurs is having the maggot blown up the line above the hook. One way to overcome this is to use an eyed hook and to put a blob of balsa cement over the eye (see Fig. 72).

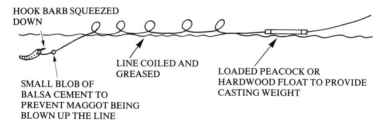

HOOK BARB SQUEEZED DOWN

LINE COILED AND GREASED

LOADED PEACOCK OR HARDWOOD FLOAT TO PROVIDE CASTING WEIGHT

SMALL BLOB OF BALSA CEMENT TO PREVENT MAGGOT BEING BLOWN UP THE LINE

*Fig. 72. Bleak rig.*

A wide top keepnet is essential to catch the fish as they are shaken off the hook, and some specialist bleak anglers connect an apron to the top so that when they shake the fish off at chest height the fish will slide down the apron into the net. It also helps to save the large number of fish that slip the hook as they are being swung in and drop between yourself and the net.

Feeding is done on a regular little and often basis, using fine wet cloud groundbait mixed with pinkies. Do not feed with hook maggots as these will quickly feed the fish off.

Often the shoal will move in and out during the session and

if you can afford the luxury of two sizes of whip, or also use your roach pole fitted with a soft flick tip, then by changing poles you can keep in touch with the fish as the range alters.

## Pole Rigs for Flowing Water

Provided the fish can be brought and held within range, the pole can be a very effective tool when fishing in flowing water, enabling the bait to be positioned and taken down very quickly to the 'hot spot' you have built up. Obviously, to achieve this loose feed is out of the question. The only way to concentrate the feed and the fish almost in front of you is by using ground bait or a bait dropper (see Fig. 75). These have a hinged flap which is secured by a weighted pin. The bait is contained in the dropper until it hits the river bed, which causes the pin to lift, releasing the flap and the contents. These are especially useful on waters which do not respond to ground bait. The term 'ground bait' is used in the loosest manner, as it does not necessarily mean bread crumb. A mixture of crumb and soil with just enough crumb to bind it can be used in situations where you do not want to over feed the fish. Hook samples can be added to provide an attractor to the fish. The mixture is used purely to get the samples quickly to the bottom, releasing them in the required area. In steady medium flows, when the fish want the bait just tripping the bottom at the speed of the current or slightly held back, a basic balsa bristle float used in conjunction with an olivette, is ideal. The set-up will be similar to the still water rig, except for the length of tail below the olivette (see Fig. 73A).

If the tackle is run through at the speed of the current, the rig shown in Fig. 70A is the one to use. The length of the tail should be between 1'6" and 2', with a No. 8 shot about 6" from the hook. The float is trimmed so that only the bristle is showing. If you find that the fish want the bait held back slightly, the float

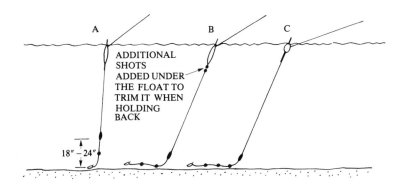

*Fig. 73. Pole fishing in flowing water.*

needs to be moved up until the olivette is just two inches clear of the bottom (see Fig. 73B). Several others can be added to the No. 8 to control the amount of lift of the tail, or in steady flows it can be split into smaller micro dust shots. These shots can be shuffled around to vary the presentation as and when conditions dictate. Often additional weight is needed on the rig to keep the shoulder of the float beneath the surface. As you hold the rig back, the float will tend to rise out of the water. One or two No. 4 shots attached to the line directly underneath the float is normally all that is needed to trim it. If you then need to revert to putting the float through with the speed of the current, these can easily be removed and the tackle re-set to its original position. In very windy conditions a long pole will wave about in the wind, preventing you from holding back smoothly due to the pole tip jerking the tackle. An AAA shot, or in extreme cases an SSG shot clipped halfway between the pole tip and the float will help to absorb the movement of the pole top (see Fig. 74). This is a very useful tip and one which can give you an edge in these situations. The same trick can be used when laying on or float legering in similar conditions. When you need to hold really hard back, or to lay on or float leger, a different pattern of float must be used. Because of its slim shape, the balsa bristle would ride too high out of the water if held back really hard. In these circumstances the pattern of float shown in Fig. 73C is needed. The body of the float is almost spherical, and the force of the water on the large area of shoulder beneath the surface helps to prevent the float from riding out of the water. When using this method, a barrel lead can be used instead of an expensive olivette.

When you need to lay on or float leger, a pole gives an obvious advantage over a rod and reel. You have much greater control of the tackle, and of course you can hold out much further across the water, ensuring you are over the edge of the shelf. When trotting through, a long length of line between pole tip and float can be used to allow you to cover a reasonable distance down the swim. When laying on or legering, only a short length of line is used in calm conditions. A longer length would only be used in windy conditions in conjunction with the large shot to cushion the sway of the pole tip (see Fig. 74).

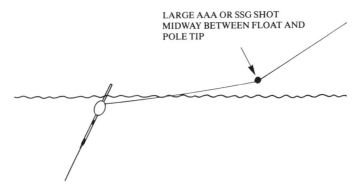

LARGE AAA OR SSG SHOT
MIDWAY BETWEEN FLOAT AND
POLE TIP

*Fig. 74. Countering pole tip movement.*

When using the paternoster rig for float legering, accurate setting of the depth is essential if the rig is to work properly. A slim balsa bristle can be used, and provided the depth is set accurately, the float is unable to lift due to the weight of the leger. Obviously the smallest leger possible is used for the prevailing conditions. This is one of the few occasions when the pole should be supported by rod rest whilst fishing, as stability of the tackle is essential for good results.

## Feeding Methods and Tactics

Although a chapter has been devoted to the methods and tactics of feeding, I have included the methods relating to pole fishing in this chapter.

As the continentals have demonstrated by their results in the world championships over the last 15 years, there is a place for the continental style bombardment tactics at the beginning of a match. I will discuss these methods, but the value and application of them can only be assessed by practical experience. There are occasions when they can be used with maggot and caster baits to good effect, but in the main it is with the use of jokers and bloodworm that they are the most effective.

The object, as with most feeding methods, is to attract and hold the fish without over-feeding. There is one rather subtle reason, other than for attraction, that such large volumes of ground bait are thrown into the swim initially. It is to ensure that regardless of the nature of the bed of the lake or river, the jokers will want to stay around the area where they were deposited. As already explained in the chapter on baits, jokers and bloodworm live naturally in water. But anything other than a silt bottom will be considered by them to be a hostile and exposed environment, so in the interests of self-preservation they will instinctively swim off in search of cover. Provided the right mix of ingredients is used in our ground bait, not only are the fish going to be attracted, but we are also creating an ideal environment for the jokers, regardless of the nature of the bottom. Fine powdered china clay, soil, silver sand and sifted peat, are all used in various combinations, depending upon the depth of water and the rate of flow, and in total will make up about 75% of the bait carrying medium. The rest is made up of various additives and particles, with some bread crumb to help bind the bait for throwing, and help it to break up slowly once it has reached the bottom. It is recommended that you experiment to find which combination of ingredients are the best to use, and which are the most effective on your own various venues. By trying these different combinations in a bath or bowl at home, you will have a complete understanding of how to achieve the required results.

Let us now look at the method of feeding. Many of the top anglers know the venue they are going to fish and make up the ground baiting medium before setting off. Normally this is done the night before the match to allow the particles to fully absorb the water. A final dampening to the required consistency is then carried out at the waterside. Other anglers prefer to mix at the waterside, using water from the venue itself. The important thing to remember is that the various ingredients should be thoroughly blended before adding the water. When the mixture has been mixed to the correct consistency and sieved to remove any lumps, the jokers are added and evenly distributed. The proportion of jokers to mixture depends upon the number of fish you think the water holds and how well you think they will feed in the prevailing conditions.

Once the whistle has gone, you must plumb around the swim and decide, having regard to the geography of the swim, where you intend to fish. Having done this, the pole must be held in its rests so that the tip and the tackle are directly over the area. Using the float tip as your marker, introduce your dozen or so cricket ball sizes of feed into the swim in a tight pattern. This should keep working for several hours and should only be topped up as and when the fall off in bite rate dictates. As you can see, it is totally contrary to normal loose feeding methods where the feeding rate is stepped up as the bite rate increases and cut back as the bite rate slows.

When using bloodworm as hook bait, a very fine wire barbless or microbarb hook must be used to prevent the fragile bait bursting. The hook point is always inserted through the greenish head, and never through the red translucent body. The bait may be fished singly or in multiples, and is always fished just off the bottom. By gently lifting and lowering the pole the bait can be made to dance invitingly above the swarm of smaller jokers.

When fishing in shallow clear canals with a wary and sparse fish population, a different medium is used to carry the loose samples to the fish. It is made up of finely sieved leaf mould and peat, and is known as 'Black Magic'. After dampening so that it will just hold together when thrown, jokers or bloodworms are added to the mix, which is designed to break up on impact with the surface of the water and form a slowly sinking black cloud into which the fish will move confidently in search of the loose samples of bait. One way to introduce loose samples of light baits such as bloodworm, squatts and pinkies accurately when using a long pole, is to use a feeding cup (see Fig. 76). This device is clipped to the end of the pole and the loose samples dropped into it. Keeping the cup upright, the pole is pushed out and when over the fishing area is tipped over by rotating the pole, and the samples are dropped into the water. They can all be tipped in together, or the cup tipped at an angle, allowing the feed to crawl out and fall into the water at intervals.

These are the specialist methods of feeding with the pole. Alternative means of feeding are centred around the traditional ways of loose feeding or ground baiting, which are fully covered in the chapter on feeding methods.

*Fig. 75. Bait dropper.*

*Fig. 76. Feeding cup clipped on pole tip.*

# 6 GENERAL TACTICS AND APPROACH

To be a successful match angler you should never go into a match unprepared. Knowledge of the venue, and complete mastery of and confidence in the methods to be used are essential. Pre-match preparation of equipment and bait must be thorough, and a plan of campaign based on up-to-date information concerning the current form of the venue needs to be decided upon. Mid-week performance of the venue is of little use if the match is to be held at the week-end. It is seldom that a venue will produce as well, or that the form will continue under match conditions. A practise session will consist of applying the information you have gathered, but using it only as a guide. If you are to stand any chance on the day, you must adapt and improve on it to give you an edge over the opposition. You must be aware that your rivals will be doing their own homework, and also realise that on the day the fish will be far less responsive than in mid-week when the banks are relatively deserted. The same methods may not work and a different bait may be needed, and the conditions on the day could be completely different. If it is a river, it may be carrying extra water or have run off extra water and be clear instead of slightly coloured. The wind may be blowing a gale or be from a different direction, or if it is winter, a severe overnight frost could cause a rapid fall in water temperatures. A practise session can only be useful when these considerations are taken into account. Quite often the experienced angler can learn more by walking the banks, getting a feel for the water, and chatting to local anglers, than by isolating himself and his thoughts by just fishing a likely looking spot. Practise sessions to the experienced matchmen mean developing new methods and tactics and perfecting them for use when conditions dictate. Using tried and tested methods, even on a new water, to the exclusion of any other considerations cannot be deemed to be practising in reality. This is one of the biggest pitfalls of the occasional match angler. He is content to bask in the pleasant memories of when everything went right, instead of analysing and correcting the mistakes he made when things went badly wrong.

Once you have made your draw and have reached your peg you must assess your swim's potential with regards to the venues current form and the prevailing conditions. On many match venues the 'Hot Spots' are well known and if you have drawn one of these it will obviously give a boost to your confidence. If you have drawn an average area, you may still stand a chance of getting into the frame if the hot spots either do not perform, or anglers of lesser ability have drawn them, although this would be more likely to happen in a club match than in an open match, as the level of ability is more varied than at open level.

If you draw in a noted poor area then you will be aiming for a section win as opposed to a match place, but the degree of commitment should still be the same. In a water with a good cross section of varied species it may only be considered poor because it lacks the match winning species such as chub or bream in sufficient quantities, but by going for roach, bleak, or gudgeon in large numbers you could still stand a chance of catching up if the larger fish do not show up on the day. The nature of the match can also dictate your tactics. If it is a large open and conditions are reasonable, then you must go for a win by fishing for the match winning species native to the water you are fishing, subject of course to you having a reasonable draw. Scratching for bits is a waste of time and opportunity if the section you have drawn has a record of producing decent weights of these fish. The methods used in this level of match fishing must be the ones that usually win, rather than the one that you enjoy fishing the most.

If you are fishing a qualifying match in a series of matches your tactics may well be different. Instead of assessing a target weight to win the match, you must assess a weight that should get you into the top ten percent if this is the proportion of anglers who will qualify for the next round. In a 200 peg match this means you need a weight that will, under normal circumstances, guarantee you a place in the top 20. If you go for a match winning species and these fail to show up then you will have failed, but if you set your stall out to catch a large quantity of small fish right from the off, then providing these are forthcoming, you should be in with a good chance. You can always change your tactics later on if you are not catching a sufficient number of these small fish, or if the anglers around you start catching the larger fish, and look like overtaking you.

Similar tactics also need to be employed in a team fishing event, fished on a points basis.

Always measure your performance with the anglers immediately around you and ignore bankside rumours. Many a match has been thrown away by anglers hearing false rumours and instead of carrying on with steadily building up a weight of small fish, panic and change methods in the hope of catching some bonus big fish that do not materialise, only to be beaten by a few bits at the weigh in.

Taking these points into consideration, and with knowledge of the conditions facing you on the day, you must work out what target weight you will need to achieve these objectives and decide whether you can achieve them with the swim you have drawn. Obviously you cannot do this accurately from the start, but by comparing your initial assessment with your actual results and the results along the match length, you can gain in experience and confidence.

During the course of the match you need to keep aware of what is happening around you without losing concentration or missing bites. You can then compare and evaluate your own performance with that of the anglers pegged immediately on either side of you. This is a much more reliable guide than taking notice of any bank side rumours. The time to check on your opposition is during 'dead' periods such as when you are retrieving your tackle or rebaiting, or at other times when your bait is not being fished and your actions are instinctive and do not require your visual attention.

The biggest enemy of the match angler is time. It is essential to save seconds at every stage of the match and to work yourself into a smooth efficient rhythm. Feeding, casting, striking, retrieving, fish removal, bait changes and tackle adjustments must all be done efficiently and without conscious thought, leaving your mind free to analyse what is going on beneath the surface. Many anglers fail to study their 'turn round' time for rebaiting or repairing tackle breakages. The time spent out of the water for these and other things such as hook changes must be analysed and improved upon if you want to be successful. This could be the edge you may have on an angler fishing next to you whose catch rate is as fast as yours, but who may take a second or two longer to get his bait back into the water. These seconds become minutes in a five hour match, and minutes may mean an extra pound of fish in the net at the end of the day. To achieve this it is important to lay out your equipment so that everything can be done with the minimum of movement and effort, and in the shortest possible time.

If you are to fish in flowing water which has a bit of colour in it, or at long range on flowing or still water, a standing position is normally the best. This allows better control of your tackle. If you are fishing at close range or on clear water where a standing position is either unnecessary or liable to frighten the fish, then a sitting position should be adopted.

The first action after you have assembled your equipment is to position your basket or seat. It needs to be far enough back from the edge of the bank to allow a good foot-hold, but not so far back as to make it necessary to stand up to land fish and put them in the keep net. Once everything is in position you should not have to stand or move around at any time during the session except when needing extra reach to control a sizeable fish in weedy or snaggy swims (see Figs. 77 – 78). The basket or seat should be stable and not be liable to tilt or move. Always carry a small trowel to use if necessary, or fit adjustable legs to your seat box.

*Fig. 77. Tackle layout for sitting position.*

Once this has been achieved you must then remove any snags around the area where your rod is to be positioned. Again moderation is the key. Do not rip out or flatten vast expanses of bank side growth or rushes. You should retain as much natural cover as possible. All that is needed is to ensure that your reel and line will not snag on anything whilst it is being held. Be as quiet as possible when carrying out these necessary tasks. Take care to keep low down and not to bump about on the bank. Never allow yourself to be silhouetted against the skyline and keep all movements slow and careful.

When the preparations have been carried out and your seat is positioned, you can move your rod and rod rests into position next to your seat, and position your keep net and landing net, ensuring that they can be reached without leaving your basket. Always position your rod rests so that the rod tip is as close to the surface of the water as possible. Bait containers, ground bait trays, spare terminal tackle, and anything else you may need during the course of the match should be positioned around you so that they can be reached comfortably. Bait containers need to be stable and unlikely to be knocked over or to tip over during the session. There should be no distractions to break your rhythm.

When the preparations are completed, your equipment set up and your bait mixed and sorted, you can give your swim a final look-over and assessment. Before the start, look around the sky and in the general direction of the wind to see if any changes in the weather are imminent. Often friendly banter with the anglers in the adjoining pegs can help break the ice and give some clues as to the potential of your area. Having said that, some anglers deliberately give misinformation to try to throw you off your stride, so do not take everything they tell you too literally.

Do not panic when the starting signal is given. Except in exceptional circumstances very little is likely to happen in the first few minutes, so it is important to find out the geography

*Fig. 78. Tackle layout for standing position.*

of your swim. This is explained fully in the relevant chapters on float fishing, legering, and pole fishing techniques. Once you have decided on your line of attack, and possibly also on a reserve line, you must start to build up your feeding and fishing rhythm, responding to any changes or making changes of your own to find and keep in touch with the fish. As already mentioned, keep an eye on what is happening around you but at the same time keep cool. Never panic if the anglers on either side of you seem to be taking an early lead. Often swims which produce early quickly dry up after a good start, but by carefully building up a slower swim, once the fish move in they will stay and settle and you will steadily build up your catch rate to the end. Often by keeping your eyes open and by adjusting the way you feed, you can take the fish away from other anglers if they are less experienced or tactically inferior to you. This is explained in the chapter on feeding methods and tactics. Remember the invisible limits of your swim as laid down in the NFA match rules. On flowing water the limit of your swim is from 1 yard upstream to within 1 yard of the angler downstream of you. On still water, half-way between yourself and the peg on either side of you, and if you have an angler opposite, half-way across the water. Provided you keep your tackle and bait within these limits you can put them anywhere in that area. Sometimes if you are using a similar method to your rivals such as feeder fishing on flowing water, or long range legering, you can negotiate an agreed extension of the upstream limit with the angler at the next peg, but if he objects then you must conform to the regulations laid down. In addition to the NFA match regulations under which most matches and club matches are fished, there may be local bye-laws and rules special to the particular stretch of water you are fishing. These may apply to the use of certain types of bait or tackle such as lead free substitutes. It is in your own interests to be aware of these and to conform to them, otherwise you risk disqualification. Normally such local rules are displayed on the match ticket or at the place of the draw at match headquarters. A summary of the current NFA regulations is given in the chapter on match administration and organisation.

# 7 FEEDING METHODS AND TACTICS

Many anglers put a great deal of thought and effort into perfecting their use of equipment, but take feeding for granted, feeding out of habit rather than with conscious thought and deliberation. They fail to realise that correct and tactical feeding is just as important as any other consideration.

To succeed, any aspiring match angler must study and experiment with his feeding until he has a full understanding of the effect resulting from the method of introduction. Not only should the amount and regularity be considered, but the timing is also important, especially in flowing waters. As well as trying to work out what the response of the fish will be, he must also judge what is happening to the feed introduced, and where and at what level it will be in the swim at any given point. He must then time the feeding, casting, and putting through of the tackle so that the hook bait is going through with the loose feed as it reaches the area of the swim where the fish are feeding. To do this he needs to be able to judge the rate of fall of the different baits through the water when the swim is being loose fed, and relate this to the rate of fall of the hook bait, which will depend upon the amount and pattern of split shot on the line. Using a glass tank or tall jug he should experiment by dropping different baits into it and timing how long they take to fall a measured foot through the water. Pale casters and commercial hook maggots take around 8 seconds to fall through a measured foot; red casters and gozzers around 10 seconds; pinkies take almost twice the time of commercial hook maggots (about 14 seconds), and hemp seed only half the time (about 4 − 5 seconds) depending on how much it has been cooked.

In flowing water, by working out the distance the flow travels per second (or ten seconds in light flows), and by taking into account the depth of the water he can work out where the feed will hit the bottom. As will be seen, if casters and hemp are being used it is necessary to keep the two separate when fishing on flowing water, throwing the hemp much further down the swim than the casters to ensure that they both collect on the bottom in the same area.

If all these considerations are taken into account it will be seen that the common practice of casting first and feeding afterwards in both still and flowing water, is completely wrong. Although bait samples are being introduced into the swim and fish will be attracted and caught, the fall or travel of the hook bait through the water is not being synchronised with that of the loose feed, and the advantage of the hook bait being taken with confidence in the flurry of activity normally generated by the fish on the sudden appearance of a number of food particles, is lost. This is particularly important when fishing for chub. As they sight a bunch of maggots coming down the swim they dive into them, snapping up as many as possible, but will often not bother to respond to just an odd sample. If by chance they do respond, they will have more time to inspect the bait, and if it behaves slightly unnaturally due to the weight of the hook or stiffness of the line, they will reject it.

The exception to this rule is when using bait samples in ground bait. In most cases this will fall through the water faster than the tackle, so its introduction can be made immediately after casting, landing in the water so that the final positioning as it reaches the bottom will coincide with the arrival of the hook bait.

We have looked at how to judge where the feed is reaching the bottom in flowing water, and in turn the reaction of the fish. Let us look again to see how this can decide what changes to tackle are needed.

Sometimes you may start to catch fish regularly, then suddenly the bites cease. Many anglers sit back thinking that the fish have 'gone off' and do nothing to find out why. One of the reasons the bites may have stopped is because the fish have moved up in the water to intercept the loose feed. This is a quite common occurrence, especially when fishing in flowing water. As they move upstream towards the angler, the fish also move up in the water following the path of the falling food. As already explained, experienced anglers are able to judge by the depth of the swim and the speed of the current just where down the swim the loose feed will hit the bottom. If they start to catch fish at the tail end of the swim and then progressively closer, and the bits slow down as the fish reach the estimated area, they will automatically 'shorten off' by moving their float closer to the hook, thereby keeping in touch with the fish. They may also 'lighten off' by moving some of the shot up towards the float to give a more natural fall of the hook bait to simulate the fall of the loose feed (see Fig. 79).

Always try to think what effect your feeding is having on the movement of the fish and try to emulate this with your hook bait

*Fig. 79. Fish rising in the water in response to loose feed.*

as well as prevailing conditions will allow. The ability to learn this will set you apart from the average angler; an essential progression if you have ambitions towards match fishing, or just wish to be a very competent angler.

As well as moving fish up from the bottom it is also possible to move fish around in the swim, or to move them into your swim from the peg downstream. If the man in the peg downstream of you is catching fish regularly and you are not, then by throwing loose feed well down your swim, and on the same line, you can bring his shoal into your swim. Having accomplished this, you must then be very careful not to allow the angler upstream to repeat the process and take them past you into his swim. For efficiency and speed try to bring the fish as close to you as possible, building up a hot spot close to the point where your tackle is under control and has reached the level in the water at which the fish are feeding. If the fish show signs of coming up beyond this point, you must introduce your feed further downstream again to prevent them passing you and moving into the next peg. The sign of this happening is normally a slowing down of the bite rate. Always keep an eye on the feeding 'line' of the anglers on either side of you, noticing the distance from the bank at which they are feeding. Once the fish are in your swim, try to slowly alter the distance you throw the feed out, so that it takes the fish either further out or closer in from you neighbours' lines. This will reduce the chance of the fish being taken from you.

These are some of the tactics which need to be considered when fishing flowing water, some of which apply to fishing still water. Timing of the fall of the feed and tackle is also important when fishing in still water, especially when the fish are taking on the drop.

What we now need to consider is the rate and amount of the

feeding. The golden rule is always to adjust the regularity and amount to the response of the fish. In fast flowing water, as the bait is being continuously swept along by the current the regularity is seldom changed, but the quantity is. This can vary from a small pinch containing five or six samples, to half a handful containing several dozen samples, the amount being controlled by the size and quantity of the fish and by the regularity of the bites. Lean times mean lean feeding, and times of plenty, regular feeding on the little and often principle.

On still waters it is a different ball game. Any feed introduced will remain on the bottom, gradually piling up unless fish are present and feeding. If you are confident of the presentation of your tackle and have made all the changes possible to encourage bites, and fish are still not forthcoming, it is because there are no fish in the swim or they are there, but are not yet feeding. When sport is slow, continuous feeding is often kept going out of habit and for something to do. But the introduction of further amounts of feed in these conditions can only have a negative effect. When the fish eventually do find their way into the swim and start to feed, the hundreds of samples of bait will be lying in an untouched heap on the bottom, and the chances of fish finding your hook bait are thus very slim. The fish will quickly fill up and then leave the swim with half the bait and your hook bait still lying there.

Always think before you throw. Consider the implications of your actions, and if in doubt, do not feed.

Tactical feeding to move fish from one swim to another is obviously far more limited on still waters, but on waters where shoals of large fish, particularly bream, are constantly moving around, it is possible. Before explaining these tactics, I want to discuss the basic pattern of ground baiting a swim on still water, as this is the method which will be under consideration.

Unless the water is known to you, the first action when the whistle blows is to establish the geography of the swim, and by using your judgement and experience, decide where you are going to introduce your feed. Assuming you are going to use leger tactics, you must cast around with your bomb, and by counting the drop of the bomb from when it hits the surface to when the tip falls back, you can establish the presence of any shelves, ledges, bars or gulleys, and then take into account water temperature, weather conditions, etc. Once the area you intend to fish has been decided upon, a couple of exploratory casts into the area are advisable before feeding. These are to check the nature of the bottom and to check whether, by any chance, the fish may already be in front of you. This will have an important bearing on how you open the proceedings. If you find there are fish there, you have a problem. The introduction of ground bait is either going to encourage them to feed or it will scare them away. I would normally change my tackle to a small swim feeder under these circumstances, introducing squatts or casters with the minimum of disturbance. If this continues to produce bites and fish, all well and good.

If after these exploratory casts there are no signs of fish being present (indicated by either sucked maggots, positive bites or line bites) then I would introduce ground bait in a diamond pattern (see Fig. 79) with the intention of laying an attractive carpet of feed on to which the fish will settle when they eventually arrive. If the main quarry are bream and if a good catch seems to be on the cards, I would start by introducing six to eight cricket ball sized offerings laced with squatts or casters and mixed to break up when the balls hit the surface. I would then put in a smaller ball of feed every 10 or 15 minutes if bites were not forthcoming. Once bites start, the feeding should stop. In cold conditions when only a few fish are likely, I would put in three or four smaller balls initially, and then leave the swim to develop.

Each successive cast can be alternated from areas B, C and D until bites start to show, giving an indication of the direction in which the fish are moving when the bites do start. You would only cast into area 'A' when bites from the other areas cease. Otherwise if you catch fish in this area whilst fish are still feeding on the closer points, you will bring a fighting fish through them, so spoiling your chances of catching more. You should always aim to take your fish from the periphery of the shoal where possible. This applies in all circumstances. Once the bites start to slow, you have the difficult decision of whether or not to put in more feed. If the anglers around you are not catching, the last thing to do is to scatter your fish and make them move into your rivals' pegs. At the same time if you do not feed, the fish will probably move on once the supply of feed is exhausted. Often a switch from a straight bomb to a small feeder can be the answer in these circumstances, but if the fish do move into adjacent pegs you must try to get them back.

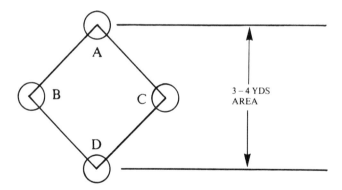

*Fig. 80. Ground baiting pattern.*

If you have lost your fish or have not had any bites, and the anglers in the adjacent pegs start to catch, you must try to encourage them to make a mistake and move the fish into your peg. In rivers such as the Welland, Witham, and Nene, you are normally fishing between the centre of the river and the far shelf. The shoals tend to move up and down the river. On large ponds or lakes they tend to move around in a circular or uneven pattern, moving further out and around the lake to find food, especially when there is angling disturbance. Unless an angler starts to ground bait heavily directly on top of a feeding shoal, the fish will settle around a quieter area, particularly if there is food present. If you are not catching and anglers on either side of you are, this is the time to top up your diamond with further balls of feed. This can often make those anglers who are catching panic, and not wishing to lose the fish to you, they will throw in balls of ground bait on top of the shoal. Provided you do not put in more bait, the fish will probably move away from this bombardment to find quieter and more attractive areas in which to feed, which hopefully will be in front of you. Provided you do not fall into the same trap, you will then start to pick off fish from around the edge of the shoal and steadily build up your weight.

Hopefully, by analysing the information in this chapter, it should give you food for thought (if you can forgive the pun). It is by learning and employing the tactics and considerations outlined that you will considerably improve upon your past performance, assuming that you are reasonably proficient at presenting your bait and tackle.

*Dave Howe celebrates the Shakespeare Superteam's success in the 1985
Angling Times/Ruddles Winter League Final. Photograph by courtesy of*
Angling Times.

*Frank Barlow with a hard earned catch taken from the River Trent in difficult winter conditions. Photograph by courtesy of* Angling Times.

*In sharp contrast, this catch taken by Stan Piecha from an in-form River Trent, earned him 2nd place in the Whitbread Championships in August 1986. Photograph by courtesy of* Angling Times.

*This catch of quality carp and bream gave Ken Giles 2nd place in the Arrow Valley Lakes Championships.*

*The moment of truth.*

*The Shakespeare Superteam with their 2nd place trophies won in the 1986 Division 5 N.F.A. National Championships. Back Row L to R: Stan Piecha, Maurice Dutfield, Ken Smith, Paul Downes, Don Slaymaker, Dave Harrel, Wayne Swinscoe. Front Row L to R: Dave Howl, Steve Webb, Ken Giles (Capt.) Dave Williams, Tony Davis.*

# 8   TEAM FISHING

Modern team fishing as we now know it is a very recent trend, and its development can be directly attributed to the dramatic impact and influence generated by the success of the Leicester Likely Lads in the late 'sixties and early 'seventies. For the first time a group of top individual anglers joined forces to fish the open circuit as a team, and dominated all of the top events, including the National Championships for a number of years until anglers from other areas, inspired by the success of the Leicester team captained by Ivan Marks, got together to provide some serious opposition.

Prior to these developments, team fishing was limited to the National Championships (a single event in those days), or to a few friends grouping together, often as an afterthought, to enter the team pool on one of the big river championships. Team selection for the National Championships was run by the individual associations on either a committee selection or a trial match basis, and this was usually the only occasion that the selected group of anglers would fish together as a team. Often the team members would differ considerably from year to year, and the only association that did field a fairly regular team over a number of years was Coventry. Led and inspired by the late Billy Lane, this consistency was rewarded with above average success in this event in the 'fifties and 'sixties.

As the proliferation of teams and match groups grew during the 'seventies, so did the number and types of team events.

Winter leagues were taken more seriously, and the big regional leagues organised by *Angling Times* became the testing grounds for many a potential National team. Many

Associations found that by having a match group that constantly fished together as a team throughout the season in both summer national knock out competitions and in the winter leagues, a much stronger and consistent team could be fielded in the National Championships, which event, as a direct reflection of the development of team fishing and match group interest, had changed from a single match decided on total weight, to 5 divisions fished on a points system. The days of the secretive individuals were numbered as the free exchange of information necessary for a group to become successful became accepted at all levels. This is reflected in the much higher and more widespread level of ability in anglers competing on the open circuit.

Despite this general increase in standards, just as it is true to say that it is the same small number of individuals that seem to be consistently at the top of the tree, so are the same small group of teams alternating with the honours in the major team competitions, and it is by no mere coincidence that the top individuals are also prominent members of the top teams. These men are mercenary anglers with tremendous commitment and will to win, and it is these qualities combined with their own strong individuality that makes them successful team anglers. To many of you this must sound contradictory, as the common trend is to suppress individuality for the sake of a "team approach". In theory this may sound right, but in practice it just does not work consistently. Match fishing, even team match fishing, is about winning. Brilliant individual performances being brought together at the end of the day to make up a brilliant winning team performance, regardless of whether they are fishing on a points or weight basis. The modern trend of building up a team of "clones" may work well on odd occasions where a single method will score on all sections, but if on the day the method fails, even in just one section, then the team will fail also. The important consideration is not consistency in method and approach, but consistency in results.

The best way I feel that I can amplify these points, is to describe to you how some teams are selected and organised, and contrast this with the way that the ''Shakespeare Superteam'' is run, with our record substantiating my beliefs.

The first impulse when selecting a team is to choose anglers who have a good record on their local waters. The problem then arises that these anglers are often geographically restricted to the methods that are commonly prevailing in that area. For example: if you are based in the south where the pole dominates, you will be looking to forming a team of top class pole anglers. This is fine if your ambitions are limited to competing in local matches and leagues. But if you intend to fish on a national as opposed to a regional basis, then this approach is a non-starter. You cannot hope to do a crash course on stick float fishing, feeder fishing or waggler fishing everytime you are drawn on an away venue and still hope to overcome the local opposition.

The top National teams consist of first class all round anglers who are open minded and adaptable. They will have mastered the principles of all aspects of the sport, and are single minded only in their personal approach and in the will to win. They are capable of assessing the swim in front of them and of using the methods best suited to getting the maximum weight from it. You cannot hope to form an instant team comprising of all these qualities immediately, unless, like myself, you have the sponsorship of a top tackle company to attract anglers of the right calibre from various parts of the country. Fortunately the rules of team angling are very loose when compared to other sports, and very few anglers are actually under contract to fish with any particular team. Providing you know exactly what and who you want, and you can obtain the backing of a good sponsor, then you can take your pick from anywhere, and any angler, even though he may be already fishing for another team, can be approached.

If, as will be more likely, you need to start from scratch, then you must only consider anglers of a good general ability who are willing to interchange knowledge and ideas to reach your ultimate standards.

They must be honest with themselves and with each other, and be as unselfish as it is possible for anglers to be in their team commitment. They must respect each other's individuality, strengths and limitations, even though they may not always agree with them. Most importantly of all they must be capable of analysing their own performance and limitations. Known trouble makers must be avoided, regardless of their ability as anglers, and team members who turn out to be continually unsettling their fellow anglers and undermining team spirit must also be dropped from the squad. Internal wrangling and flag flying at the expense of harmony will always undermine any chance of success.

The next most important consideration is the age range. Ideally a team should consist of members of a mixed age group, but with a strong core of mature anglers. This is not necessarily to ensure a large concentration of experience, although this is an additional consideration. The main reason is that the more mature members will invariably have a more settled life style, with less demands and distractions upon their personal and financial commitment. A successful young single angler can suddenly become a liability if he has to change his priorities due to the demands of having to save for his wedding and needing to spend more time with his fiancée. He will find that his loyalties are split, and naturally his performance will suffer as a consequence. The same thing can happen to a newly married man who is starting a family. Pools, transport and bait expenditure have to take second place to prams, cots and baby clothes, unless he has a very understanding wife, can regularly supplement his income with his match winnings, and can time the happy event to coincide with the closed season. External pressures such as these affect confidence and performance and once this spiral begins it is very difficult to reverse it. These then are the major points to consider when recruiting members for a team or match group. Having brought the anglers together, how should they be organised and moulded together into an effective winning team?

Some people advocate group discussion, group selection and group decision as the best ways of achieving group performance and success. As an ideal it may seem a sensible approach, but in reality it just will not work. Instead of producing success, all it will generate is hot air and confusion. Anyone who has attended a group meeting of this type will know that if as much effort and energy was put into performance on the bankside as is put into the arguing and debating at these meetings, then no one could touch them in a contest.

Team selection and performance must be the responsibility of just one person. If the team fails to win then it is that person's responsibility. He makes the decisions and all that the anglers he has selected need to worry about is doing their best on the day.

The nature of angling and of anglers is such that lack of success can always be passed off by blaming the venue and the conditions. But in a well disciplined team, the team captain or manager knows that if the team has failed it is because it was not good enough. He will accept this as his responsibility, as it was he who selected the team, and the team in turn will accept that they fished badly without having to be told. On this basis they will analyse what went wrong without apportioning blame, and be stronger for it.

Team selection should always be on a basis of "horses for courses". No member should have the right to automatic selection, not even the captain. When deciding his team he will select those best suited to the venue and the conditions, and take into account their current individual form in the weeks previous to the match. Someone who is on a winning streak will be on a high as regards his confidence, and must always be considered in preference to an angler who is having a bad run. At no time should the captain or manager have to justify his decision and all the squad members should respect this. This may seem a very dictatorial way of running a team but it is, I am certain, the only way. If an angler gives me his £5 stake for the team pool I am obligated to getting him a return on his investment, and I can only do that by fielding our strongest team and winning the match.

Team plans should always be as flexible as possible, and conditions of approach should never by imposed upon team members. They must be free at all times to decide upon or change their methods when they reach their swim. Team plans are seldom of any use except as a very loose guide. If anglers feel constrained and unable to respond to their natural instincts, they cannot fish effectively. Team spirit is fine in the club house or at the draw and especially in the pub after the match, but once each individual angler reaches his peg he is totally on his own.

This does not mean to say that the Shakespeare Superteam does not have meetings or discussions about tactics. We do, but we keep them to the necessary minimum. These will normally consist of a brief chat before and after the draw, where we clue in any members of the team who are relatively new to the venue, as to what type of swim they have drawn, and of possible ways of approach that have produced recently in similar conditions. We do not dictate to or impose our knowledge on to other team members, but we do encourage interchange of ideas and suggestions between ourselves, and on those very rare of occasions I feel that some members of the team may be tactically weaker than others on a particular venue or method, then I must remedy this as subtly as possible. Rather than directly pointing this out to them and then instructing them on what to do, I prefer to casually suggest to them that they have a word with so and so, as he has had a great deal of experience and success either on the water or of using the method, and then be confident that the anglers in question will be keen enough in their commitment to ask, and that the advice that they receive will be sound.

One of the rare times that we have a formal team meeting is to discuss the tactics and approach for the National Championships. We normally practise on the venue during the last 3 weeks that the water is open to contestants for practise, and then during the week before the match we hold our meeting. This is usually an informal but disciplined affair where we go around the table and each member says his piece, describing his experiences during the practise sessions and what he found to be the most successful methods.

Slowly but surely a pattern will emerge over the various sections, and once all the information has been kicked around it is then my job as captain to analyse all the points and then to agree an approach with the team members. This will always be just a basic approach, with a safety valve built in, allowing any team member to abandon it and to follow his instincts as and when the situation dictates. Many teams insist upon their members virtually living on the venue all season before the match and hold umpteen meetings prior to the event. This I feel must have a negative influence, as the team will get sick of seeing the venue, and the meetings will tend to get bogged down, with the result that enthusiasm falls off in the weeks running up to the match instead of being generated upwards.

I feel certain that our team has the correct approach to this situation. By allowing the team members to fish their normal calendar of matches and events during the season, they will prepare for the run up to the National in a relaxed and confident manner, completely happy to give me their undivided commitment for the last few weeks. This will also bring a fresh and open minded attitude to the whole affair.

If the venue is quite a distance from their normal fishing grounds, then this freshness gives us an even greater advantage. A team that has had to travel long distances every weekend for months at a time will be very run down both physically and mentally, and unless some form of regular success, spread throughout the team, has been forthcoming to compensate for the missed opportunities, whether real or imagined, that have been lost locally as a result of this, then morale will be seriously undermined. Even if they are reasonably successful on the day, many of them will still consider that the price will have been too high.

The captain's role apart from team selection and organisation, is to maintain unity, spirit and discipline within the team.

Discipline is essential, despite what some people would consider to be an over generous amount of tactical freedom. However, this should not be just the discipline of accepting the captain's decision without question, but also self-discipline. Honesty and trust are also very important. These are the things that generate real team spirit.

Any angler must be prepared to drop himself from the team if he feels that for any reason he cannot perform to the best of his ability on the day. He must also have the courage to admit that he has fished badly, even when his result seems acceptable. A top class angler does not accept congratulations for weighing in fifteen pounds for a third place, when he knows in his heart he should have caught twenty pounds for a win.

Because of this high level of commitment and self discipline in the Shakespeare Superteam, it is very rare that disciplinary action has to be taken against any of our team members. On those few occasions that I have had to give anyone a dressing down, it has always been done privately and never in front of any of the other team members. The timing and nature of this also depends on the individual concerned, but it never pays to discipline anyone just prior to a match for obvious reasons. If, following a telling off or because he has not been picked for a number of matches a team member shows dissent, then he will be dropped from the squad. The attitude of any good team angler should be to work harder and to get himself back into form if his selection is being continually overlooked. He should analyse his past performance honestly and go all out with the intention of earning his place back into the team.

### Knockout Competitions

I have described the general approach to team fishing that can be applied to most types of league and national events, but one exception to normal policy that needs to be considered is the approach to knockout competitions fished on a home and away basis.

As this type of competition is becoming increasingly popular, and as more and more teams are being formed with these events in mind, then I feel that I must cover this aspect of team fishing.

Let us first deal with fishing on a home venue. Unless you feel confident that your team can compete with the strongest of opposition, then the main consideration when choosing a home venue is to select a water that does not respond well to usual methods or baits. The team must then practise on the water and perfect the method to be used. This is one of those rare occasions when it pays a team to adopt specialist "clone fishing" tactics. The object is to get well ahead of the opposition before they twig the method, by which time it will be too late for them to catch up.

The away team will of course try to do some homework and get some practise in on the water prior to the match, so it is important that you find a venue and a method that cannot be easily mastered by the opposition with just a brief visit or by analysing local knowledge.

The real problem is of course that you will be at this same disadvantage when you go to an away venue, especially if you have drawn against a really top class team. Often, if this should happen, it may pay the team to chance fishing specialist baits for big fish if it is for example to be held on a lake that contains carp or tench as well as the more general match species. You need to weigh up the odds and the opposition. If you are unlikely to beat the team under normal circumstances by fishing conventional match methods, then you will be unlikely to beat them on their own water that way. Therefore an extreme approach may be the only way of winning. Perhaps only a couple of you may catch, but the total weight could be more than the oppositions total, and if it does not pay off you can at least console yourself with the fact that you would not have beaten them anyway by using normal methods.

It is seldom that we have to resort to these extremes as we are fortunate in having a team of top class anglers who can compete on most waters using traditional methods, but even we have been known to come unstuck against opponents of lesser ability, who have used similar tactics to those I have outlined. Having said that I can recall one very memorable occasion whereby we scuppered an opponent's plans of succeeding with these tactics by saturating the water with thousands of pieces of luncheon meat in the opening minutes of the match, feeding off the big fish and scraping home with a few pounds of bits. Not a very friendly tactic I know, but one that worked and that underlines the determination and will to win that must be employed if you intend to succeed.

# 9 TOP TWENTY HINTS AND TIPS

**Preventing over-casts when fishing the far bank** *by Ken Giles*
Over-casting can be a serious problem when you have to fish tight against the far bank. The resultant breakages cost valuable minutes, and the steady feeding and casting rhythm you have built up will be broken, spoiling your chances of building up a steady catch rate. One way of overcoming this is to cast out initially to the required position, then fit a broad elastic band over the spool of your reel. This will ensure that on subsequent casts the elastic band will prevent further line being pulled off your spool, and the braking effect will cause your tail to straighten out and fall through the water in a straight line, ready to indicate the slightest bite.

**Protecting loose hooks** *by Frank Barlow*
Most matchmen buy their hooks in plastic containers of 50. The problem then arises of either spillage whilst opening the container, or of rust appearing on the hooks during the course of the season. One simple and effective way of overcoming these problems is to put a thin smear of vaseline inside each container. This will prevent both rusting and spillage of hooks, and also lubricate the line whilst whipping them up and helping to prevent damage to the line when tightening the whipping. This is very important when using the very fine hook lengths essential to modern match fishing methods.

**Fishing the pole . . . out of your depth?** *by Stan Piecha*
Many anglers are out of their depth when it comes to pole fishing.

It's not that they fail to handle the equipment properly, but that they overlook the most vital factor in this increasingly important branch of the sport . . . plumbing the depth. Watch any World Championship, the top Continentals and the England team members will spend as long as 15 minutes working out the contours of the bottom of the river or lake, before selecting their mark to fish.

The secret is to look for a ledge (see dia.), which would be a natural patrolling route for feeding fish. If there is no ledge, and the bed just continues to drop at a sharp angle, go for the area where it finally flattens down to a uniform depth.

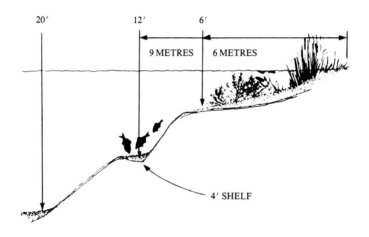

This extra time spent working out the contours of the bottom won me the £3000 top prize in last year's King of Clubs Championship.

On paper, the swim was a duff one, but after careful plumbing I discovered that at six metres it was 6' deep, gradually shelving off to 12' at 9 metres. By putting another section onto the pole, I was able to 'feel' around and find that 12' ledge was 4' wide. Then it dropped off to 20', too deep to hold any real number of fish.

The ledge I had discovered was a natural holding spot and, by fishing at 9 metres with a very short line between float and pole tip, I was able to drop my hookbait and ground bait onto the spot every time. I won the match with 45lb of bream . . . on a peg that had previously produced a combined, two-day weight of 6lb!

**Brush up your reel's performance** *by Ken Giles*
With use, reels both open and closed face get clogged with dried groundbait, mud, etc. Obviously they work best if cleaned regularly. However, this is usually a time consuming and fiddley job, but I have found the ideal tool for it – an old toothbrush. The bristles are stout enough to remove any foreign bodies from the reel, yet soft enough not to cause damage.

**Sinking the line at distance** *by Steve Webb*
I'm sure most of you are aware of the need to sink your line, when adverse wind conditions would otherwise drag your float tackle in what, from a fish's point of view, would be an unnatural movement.

Many anglers cast beyond their chosen area, dip the rod tip into the water and give a few sharp turns of the reel to sink the line.

This usually works well enough, but what happens when you want to cast to a feature on the far bank and keep your tackle in that position? Turning the reel obviously retrieves line, which in turn drags your tackle back towards you.

What I do in such conditions is cast to the chosen position on the far bank, dip the rod tip under the water (the further the distance, the deeper the rod tip) and snatch the rod sharply up till it just clears the water. This quickly sinks the line without dragging your tackle out of position.

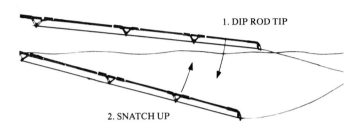

**Visible benefits on the stick float** *by Wayne Swinscoe*
When stick float fishing, the float itself must be 'shotted down' (approx ⅛″ showing) for perfect presentation. Therefore, with so little float above the surface, it is vital that the right coloured top is chosen for good visibility.

On wide rivers with very little bankside cover, like the Trent, black is the preferred colour. But for tree-lined venues, such as the Warwickshire Avon or the Thames, bright orange or yellow is more appropriate. But, as we all know, conditions in angling change rapidly sometimes, making the float difficult to see. To counter these changes, waterproof felt-tip pens can be used to alter the colour of your float top, making the float visible again with no change to your float rig.

**Closed-face line guide** *by Dave Williams*
When using closed-face reels, never overfill the spool with line, as this causes more casting problems than an underfilled spool. Use this as a guide to more effective fishing.

**Match reels spools:** Double rubber fishing, i.e. stick and balsa float – 50/60yds of line. Waggler and light legering – 70/80yds of line.

**Don't get frozen out!** *by Dave Howl*
How many times when fishing in winter have your rod rings frozen, making it impossible to fish correctly? Well, one simple way around it is to buy an eye-dropper from your local chemist and fill it with glycerine. Then, before you start fishing, put a spot of it into every rod ring. You'll be amazed at the difference it makes. The glycerine prevents ice forming on the rings and allows you to fish properly, while anglers around you are struggling.

**The business end of the gear** *by David Harrell*
It never ceases to amaze me how many anglers will spend hundreds of pounds to obtain the best equipment, but neglect the business end of the tackle – hook and line. Fine lines deteriorate quickly and should be changed regularly. I always change my floating lines after about 20 hours' fishing. For the minimal cost involved, I consider this to be well worthwhile. After all, a breakage while playing a match-winning fish can prove much more costly.

I use Shakespeare Omni line and for most of my float work, I find the 2lb breaking strain perfectly adequate. For heavier float fishing, I use Omni 2.5lb.

Hook patterns are very much a matter of personal choice; but, here again, many anglers do tend to use lines that are far too heavy, or too light, for the particular type of hook they are using. For example, it's no use whatsoever tying a fine wire, size 24 hook to 4lb line. Similarly, a size 8 will not lend itself to being tied to 1lb line. As a general guideline, I tie all my fine wire hooks (24 – 20) to 1lb Omni, medium wire hooks (20, 18, 16) to 1.5lb Omni and forged hooks (20, 18, 16, 14) to 2lb. I recommend at least a dozen turns on the hook shank and a minimum hook length of 2'. This allows for maximum stretch, if a large fish is encountered.

### Silicone secrets *by Tony Davis*
One of the most useful items in my tackle box is a small aerosol of Shakespeare silicone oil, which was originally produced for the trout angler to make dry flies float. I spray this on my spools of float fishing line to make the line float high on the surface, giving more efficient line control and striking. A little sprayed on the joints of catapult rubber makes them last much longer. While yet another use is to spray pole elastic to protect and lubricate it and make it run freely from the end of the pole. Pole joints can also benefit from a quick spraying after cleaning, especially the joints of telescopic poles, whips, or landing net handles. Since I started to use it I have never had a joint stick or jam up on me.

### Feeder fishing for chub *by Maurice Dutfield*
First of all, the feeder must be loaded with the correct weight so that it just holds bottom. Then cast slightly upstream, so that it takes hold directly opposite to you. Now position the rod high and pointing downstream to keep most of the line off the water and form the all important bow, that allows the use of small hooks (20 – 22 barbless) and light bottoms (1.5 – 2.0lb). When you get a bite, don't strike – just simply lift the rod, as the fish usually hooks itself.

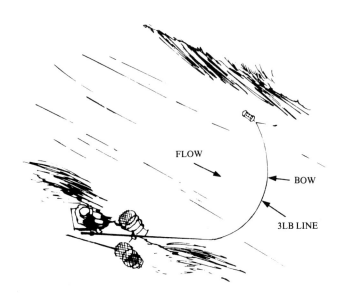

**Better bait** *by Frank Barlow*

I think that just about the most important thing in angling is bait; for, quite simply, without it you can't catch fish! So always make sure your bait is completely fresh in every way. Scour maggots thoroughly in coarse bran to clean and slightly soften them. Take them to the bank in fresh maize meal.

Casters too should always be fresh – never save them in water, as this just suffocates them and sours them. Always keep an eye on your groundbait, as this can go off, like anything else. Store it in a dry, cool place on a wooden board, to keep it in peak condition.

**Extra rubber** *by Paul Downes*

When using a stick or balsa float 'top and bottom', always use three rubbers. Then, if one breaks, there is no need to dismantle the tackle completely to carry on fishing.

Also, when moving the float up or down the line, lubricate the float with saliva. This prevents friction which can dramatically weaken the line.

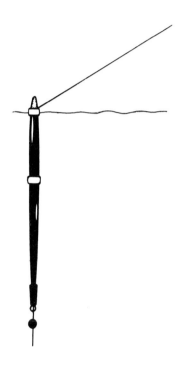

**Extra buoyancy for pole floats** *by Paul Downes*
When shotting up delicate pole floats for bloodworm fishing, it is essential to leave only a fraction of the bristle showing to indicate delicate bites from small fish. The extreme sensitivity of bristle tips means this is often difficult to do. However, by

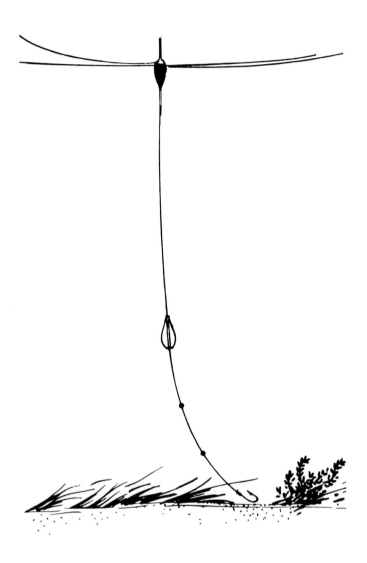

slightly overshotting the float and then smearing it lightly with vaseline to add buoyancy it is always possible to get the required float setting.

### Finding the joint *by Don Slaymaker*

When fishing the pole with a short line, I always put a piece of white tape about one inch above the joint of the pole that I am going to be taking apart. This saves me a lot of time looking for the joint during the match.

Another handy pole fishing tip is to set up a "Pole Roller" behind you on the bank, as this allows the pole to travel back more quickly and prevents damage to it.

### Stiff joints *by Ken Giles*

The joints on carbon rods and poles are of fairly soft material. After a bit of use, when you're putting these joints together you'll often hear a grating noise. This is due to small particles of sand or grit becoming lodged in the joints. If you just carry on forcing the joint home, you eventually end up with very loose joints. I have found that the answer to this, as soon as you first hear the grating sound, is to pull the joint apart and dip the female section in the water to a depth of about 3 or 4 inches, and swish it about to dislodge any foreign matter. Remember in winter to wipe the joints dry to prevent freezing.

### Poles Apart *by Dave Williams*

There is absolutely no reason to have problems with sticking joints, when using long, take-apart poles. Simply fix PVC tape or shrink tube to the male joints about 2mm above the female section, when the joint is firmly in position. This will prevent you engaging the joints too deeply onto the taper and causing them to stick. This system can be further developed by using different coloured tape or tube for each joint, to provide a foolproof guide when breaking down the pole. This concept can be further improved by using the same colour of pole float winder as each tape to give the correct line length.

**Tip for chips** *by Dave Howl*
One of the most important items in the angler's armoury are his floats, each one designed to do a different job under different conditions. However, such a simple thing as a chip in the paintwork can allow water to get into the float and completely upset its balance, making it useless at vital times.

Now, I know that matchmen particularly, sometimes carry as many as a hundred floats, so to check every one frequently would be very tiresome. A simple and effective way round this problem is to carry a bottle of clear nail varnish in your tackle box. Then, if you choose a float with a chip in it, it's simple to apply a blob of varnish, which dries quickly to leave your float as good as new.

**Making the most of the tube** *by Steve Webb*
Silicon tubing has many more uses than just as a mere float attachment.

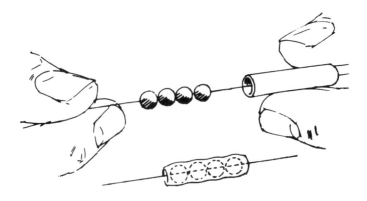

For example, when fishing swift flowing water, a bulk of shot in close proximity to the hook is often vital. These shots can have an annoying habit of curling up and twisting the line. To obviate this, just slide a piece of silicon tubing of suitable diameter and length over the group of shot.

Additionally, if light conditions change when float fishing, slide a length of black silicon tube over the coloured tips of wagglers for a quick change to a black float top.

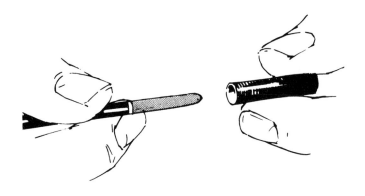

**Floaters** *by Wayne Swinscoe*
Here's a simple idea that will help you catch a few more fish on venues where you're expecting to catch on the drop or in mid water with maggot as bait. The night before your planned session, cover the bottom of a small bait container with water, about half an inch deep. Add a couple of handfuls of clean maggots, enough for hookbait. After half an hour, dry and clean the maggots off in maize meal, after this treatment the maggots should float, but when used on the hook, they sink slowly at the same speed as the loose feed and look more natural and acceptable to the fish.

# 10 MATCH ADMINISTRATION AND RULES

As explained in the introduction, there are three main levels of match fishing. Firstly there is the club level where matches are fished either on club waters, or are booked on other waters to which the club members will travel by bus or shared transport. Secondly there are open matches run by large clubs and associations, and as the title suggests, are open to any angler regardless of ability and which are subject only to the purchase of a ticket. Finally there are invitation matches run by sponsors of various related or unrelated products, to which top anglers are invited, or other anglers qualify for by winning places in a series of open matches. In addition there are a number of team events such as the National Championships, and Winter League and Summer Knock-Out competitions, which require anglers to apply to either clubs or associations for selection to the team.

The level of competition can vary from one area to another, and from one club to another, but with the ease of modern travel most open events of one hundred pegs or more will attract a few top men and many first class local anglers. Club events of 30 or 40 pegs will generally have a lower standard of opposition, with perhaps a couple of club cracks to watch out for, although some top clubs in my area have a much higher than usual standard of opposition, which is also more widely spread through the membership, making for some very good matches.

Most matches are published in association or club membership books, as well as in the forthcoming match columns in the weekly angling press. Posters are also circulated to tackle shops. Tickets can be applied for, or booked by telephone, and often a limited number are available from the organisers on the day. These days the tickets are often 'all-in', which means the pools are included in the cost, ensuring a good pay-out. If the ticket is for match entry only, separate pools are offered on the day. These normally consist of three categories – winner takes all, which is self-explanatory; match place pools which can be paid for first, second, third and sometimes fourth and fifth match places, and a section pool paid to the winner of each section, and sometimes to the second or third place in a section. Most matches are fished in sections to give everyone a chance to win something even if they have drawn a poor area of the venue. All pools must be paid before drawing your peg. Always carry a pen or pencil when you go to a match so that you can fill in your pools card and peg card without holding up the proceedings. When you have drawn, you then proceed to your peg. Most matches are fished under N.F.A. rules, and on occasions also to additional special association or club rules relating to bait restrictions or the use of lead free weights. These rules are normally printed on the tickets. Infringement of any of these rules or regulations can leave you open to disqualification. A summary of the main N.F.A. rules is as follows:

1. Each competitor on drawing their number shall proceed to the corresponding number on the bank and this will be considered their fishing ground where they will fish. THE PEG MUST REMAIN IN POSITION UNTIL THE WEIGH-IN IS COMPLETED.

2. No form of container for preserving the catch other than a keepnet can be used. Keepnets must be not less than 1.5 metres in length. Circular nets must not be less than 35 cms. in diameter, rectangular nets not less than 35 cms x 30 cms. Only knotless mesh nets are permissible. Competitors must take every practicable step to keep their fish alive, and after weighing them must ensure their careful return to the water. If for any reason fish are seen to be in distress, a competitor or match official has the right to demand that they be

weighed immediately and returned to the water during the course of the match.

3. A competitor must use only one rod and line at any one time but may have other rods and tackles assembled for use provided such other tackles are not baited. On the tackle in use the angler must not have more than one single hook. No treble or double hooks of any kind are permitted.

4. Any bait can be used except live or dead fish, frogs, spinning baits or artificial lures.

5. No competitor shall have live or dead fish in their possession before a match. All competitors must submit to a search if requested by a contest official.

6. No competitor may groundbait or loose feed the swim, wet a line, plumb the depth or disturb the water in any way before the signal, other than to wet groundbait, clear their fishing ground of weed or obstruction, or to position their keepnet(s).

7. A competitor must strike, play and land their own fish.

8. An angler can wade, other than for the purpose of positioning their keepnet(s), provided they remain within one yard of the water's edge.

9. No competitor shall leave their peg at any time during the course of the match other than to answer the call of nature, and then they must not leave their baited hook in the water. At the end of the match a competitor must remain at the peg until their catch has been weighed, unless they have been detailed for weighing duties. Any competitor so detailed must have a witness to the weighing of their own catch.

10. A competitor must cease fishing at the finishing signal. Should they still be playing a fish hooked before the signal is given, they will be permitted 15 minutes after time has been called, to land the fish.

11. Competitors are responsible for ensuring that their pegs are clear of litter, and no competitor may have their catch weighed in who has litter lying on the banks of their swim.
12. All the foregoing rules are subject to the bye-laws of the Water Authority in whose area the competition is being fished.

Any complaints or disputes must be reported to the officials immediately after the match. If you arrive at your swim and consider it unsuitable, you must not reposition your peg without the permission of a match official. Unsuitable or dangerous pegs due to the nature of the bank, or because of low overhead power cables, must be reported, and you are entitled to redraw provided there are spare pegs left. Once you are in your peg you must observe its boundaries. You are allowed to fish within 1 yard either side of the actual peg post or ticket. The tackle limits are as follows. On flowing water, from one yard upstream to within one yard upstream of the lower peg, and where both banks have been pegged, the centre of the river, though normally this is a rare occurrence. On still water you can fish up to halfway between your peg and the pegs on either side of you. When feeder fishing you may wish to cast further upstream than the one yard allowed. This is only possible if you can reach some private agreement with the angler upstream of you. If he objects you must respect the boundaries. When fishing drains or rivers which are controlled by sluice gates, the still water boundaries will apply whilst the water is static, but the flowing water boundaries will apply when it starts to pull off. The normal minimum distance of pegging is 15 yards, but on natural rivers this can often be much greater. On permanently pegged rivers such as the Witham, the pegging is very tight.

If you are in any doubt about rules which apply to a particular match, always get clarification from a match official before the draw.

# READER NOTES

| DATE: | VENUE: | REMARKS |
| --- | --- | --- |
| | | |

| DATE: | VENUE: | REMARKS |
| --- | --- | --- |
|  |  |  |

| DATE: | VENUE: | REMARKS |
|-------|--------|---------|
|       |        |         |

| DATE: | VENUE: | REMARKS |
|-------|--------|---------|
|       |        |         |

| DATE: | VENUE: | REMARKS |
|-------|--------|---------|
|       |        |         |